MW01040346

THE FORERUNNER OF THE SPLIT-BAMBOO

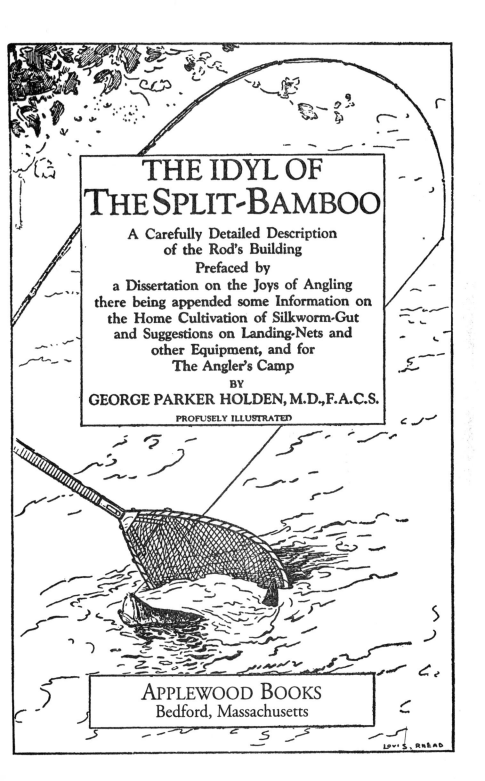

THE IDYL OF
THE SPLIT-BAMBOO

A Carefully Detailed Description
of the Rod's Building
Prefaced by
a Dissertation on the Joys of Angling
there being appended some Information on
the Home Cultivation of Silkworm-Gut
and Suggestions on Landing-Nets and
other Equipment, and for
The Angler's Camp

BY

GEORGE PARKER HOLDEN, M.D., F.A.C.S.

PROFUSELY ILLUSTRATED

APPLEWOOD BOOKS
Bedford, Massachusetts

The Idyl of the Split-Bamboo was originally published in 1920 by
Stewart & Kidd Company of Cincinnati, Ohio.

ISBN 1-55709-492-6

Thank you for purchasing an Applewood Book.
Applewood reprints America's lively classics—books
from the past that are of interest to modern readers.
For a free copy of our current catalog, write to:
Applewood Books, P.O. Box 365, Bedford, MA 01730.

---

10 9 8 7 6 5 4 3 2 1

Library of Congress Catalog Card Number: 98-86201

This Anglers' Book
is Dedicated
first of all, to
THAT DEAR WOMAN
who "lets me;"
next, to the memory of a friend,
SIDNEY HUGHES
— a quiet and gentle
son of his loved southland,
where he dropped asleep —
wizard with a fly, and
to whom i owe my first
introduction to trouting;
and, after these,
to that genial coterie of
CHERISHED COMPANIONS
with whom it has been my good fortune
to have spent some of the most
joyous hours of my life
out-o'-door

FOREWORD

The publishers regret that on account of Dr. van Dyke's unexpected absence abroad, this "Foreword" has to consist of the following letter instead of the introduction which we were anticipating. But if this distinguished angler's prediction concerning the present volume proves correct, perhaps we can have that introduction in a later edition.

Avalon
Princeton, N. J.
December 8, 1919

Dear Dr. Holden:

I am glad to hear about your new book on "The Split-Bamboo Rod," and though I had made a resolve not to write any more introductions for books, or in fact undertake any additional work of any kind this winter and spring, I cannot resist the impulse to make an exception in your case, because I feel sure that your book will be a valuable addition to the practical literature of angling, as well as a delightful record of the inward and outward joys of that art. If therefore you will send me a set of page proofs of the book when it is finished, I shall be very glad to try my hand at a little " Foreword," although I know that your volume will not need any introduction.

Believe me,
Cordially yours,
HENRY VAN DYKE

PREFACE

We sing the song of the Split-Bamboo.

The author's previous book, *Streamcraft,* deals mainly with actual streamside technic — the selection, care, rigging, and use of the rod; with the choosing of lures, natural and artificial, and their manipulation; and with fly-tying. Its contents, presented in a pocket form, well adapt it for a ready-reference companion on fishing expeditions and even when actually engaged on the water in the quest of the finny game. It comprises much data correlated from many sources, though always authoritative. But nowhere else, to his knowledge, may guidance be found for the construction of the Split-Bamboo Rod equally comprehensive and detailed as in the pages that follow. This has been preceded by a dissertation on " The Joys of Angling," and there has been appended some information on " Cultivating Silkworm-Gut at Home," and some suggestions on " Landing-Nets and Other Equipment," and for " The Angler's Camp." The former treatise is largely a working manual for the open season and the stream; this is more a book for Winter evenings and the fireside, and for the workshop.

The sportsman's transcendent implements are his rod and his gun.   Compared with the glut of " gun-dope "— data on models, actions, bores, sights, gauges, shells, ballistics, etc.— constantly appearing in the outdoor journals and in book form for the consumption of the followers of Nimrod, there is a dearth of readily-available and plain technical information relating to the fishing-rod.   While it might be urged that comparatively but few anglers would care to undertake the manufacture of this instrument in its glorified form, it requires little argument to convince anyone that fishermen in general, whether especially addicted either to fresh or salt water, love to tinker with their tackle; and no argument at all to elucidate that a treatise dealing with construction must perforce include full directions for all rod renovation and repairs.   He that can make a rod certainly can fix one.   Further, we admit the temerity to trust that this book will appreciably stimulate an increase in the number of those who will be emboldened to essay the " whole trick."

Building a split-bamboo rod is an operation, and we have explained our technic with the same conscientious care that we would observe in delineating the consecutive details of a surgical operation; for it is a matter of curious comment that amongst all we have read of definite instruction in this art, we never received any help from such sources in overcoming those particular difficulties in handling and working bamboo which at first gave us the most trouble; perversely, as it seemed — albeit including much of interest and of value — these authorities told us everything except what *we* most needed to know for perfect success, and at just such critical places they left us stranded. We earnestly hope to succeed here in obviating a like criticism.

While some of the subjects discussed in these volumes have been dealt with much more exhaustively in various other and ofttimes sumptuous and expensive treatises — many of them of foreign authorship — it has been the present writer's ambition to condense between the two pairs of covers more information than hitherto has appeared within the same extent of text, of essential, practical interest to the American fresh-water fisherman, and to the average type of enthusiastic American trout-fisherman of today in particular; and at the same time not without some flavor of the delightful literary, esthetic, and what may be termed the Nature sides of angling, which have inseparably been associated with the sport from the beginning. In this way it is hoped that the novice may easily attain an adequate idea of the comprehensive scope of his artful recreation, while our efforts shall not prove without interest even to those who have a more familiar acquaintance with the " tight line."

With appreciation we acknowledge our indebtedness to Mr. Edwin T. Whiffen of New Rochelle,

N. Y., and to the *Forest and Stream* magazine, for
the use of Mr. Whiffen's delightful bit of natural history comprised in Chapter XI.

That " good luck " in abundant measure may attend the reader, is the greeting of

A BROTHER ANGLER

Yonkers, N. Y., *Winter, 1919–20*

CONTENTS

ILLUSTRATIONS

And numerous additional cuts mainly illustrative of the technical text, some being from diagrammatic sketches by the author

[1] This flashlight of doe and fawns is one of four pictures by Mr. Shiras exhibited at the Paris Exposition by the U. S. Government and receiving the Gold Medal; and it was again exhibited at the World's Fair in St. Louis, being awarded the Grand Prize.

THE JOYS OF ANGLING

THE IDYL OF THE SPLIT-BAMBOO

CHAPTER I

THE JOYS OF ANGLING

Now, when the first foul torrents of the brooks,
Swell'd with the vernal rains, is ebb'd away,
And, whitening, down their mossy-tinctured stream
Descends the billowy foam; now is the time
To tempt the trout. The well-dissembled fly,
The rod fine-tapering with elastic spring,
Snatch'd from the hoary steed the floating line,
And all thy slender watery stores prepare.
. . . .
When with his lively ray, the potent sun
Has pierced the streams and roused the finny race,
Then, issuing cheerful, to thy sport repair.
Chief should the western breezes curling play,
And light o'er ether bear the shadowy clouds.
High to their fount, this day, trace up the brooks;
The next, pursue their rocky-channel'd maze
Down to the river, in whose ample wave
Their little Naiads love to sport at large.

THOMSON'S *Seasons*

Fresh- or sweet-water angling is one of the most ancient, cleanest, most engrossing, enduring, healthful, and accessible of recreations available in this world of mingled riches and poverty, pleasure and pain, of steadfast affections and changing regard; and it possesses a considerable literature, both delightful and classical, extending from before the times of Dame Juliana Berners, prioress of Sopwell nunnery, and of its patron saint Izaak Walton, down to the present day. "Bards have sung its praises, traditions have hallowed it, and philosophers have reveled in the gentle pastime, since the days of Oppian and Homer." Need we say here for the enlightenment of anyone that Walton is the immortal author of "a discourse on fish and fishing not unworthy the perusal of most anglers," the same being, as another famed angling writer aptly has characterized it, "a conglomeration of fertile meadows, crystal brooks, meandering streams, milk-maids' songs, and moral reflections," which down through the years has continued to "prove irresistible."

Perhaps the reader may now be curious to know something of what the good Dame Berners had to say of "fysshynge", in the year 1500 A. D.—"Dowteles thene folowyth it, that it must be the dysporte of fysshynge with an angle. For all other manere is also laborous, and grevous, whych many tymes hath be seen cause of grete infirmytes. But the angler may have no colde, nor no dysease nor angre, but if he be causer hymself. For he may not lese at the moost but a lyne or an hoke: of whych he may have store plentee of his owne makynge, as this symple treatise shall teche him. So, thenne, his losse is not greous, and other greffes may he not have, savynge but yf ony fisse breke away after that he is take on the hoke; or elles that he catche nought; which been not greous. For yf he dooth as this treatyse techyth, but yf there be nought in the water, and yette atte the leesth he hath holsom walke and mery, at his ease: a swete ayre of the swete savours of the mede floures, that makyth hym hungry. He hereth the melodyous armony of foules. He seeth the yonge swannes; heerons; duckes; cotes, and many other foules wyth theyr brodes; whyche me seemyth better than alle of noyse of houndys; the blastes of hornys and the crye of foulis that hunters, faukeners and foulers can make. And yf the angler take fysshe: surely thenne is there noo man merier than he is in his spyryte."

In 1919 Emerson Hough comments at sixty-three: " By process of elimination, I have found a great many other sorts of sport of late to be too hard or too easy or too clean or too dirty. . . . Indeed, what really can equal the art of the fly-rod on a good trout-water? It is clean, it is beautiful beyond compari-son, it is difficult and yet alluring. . . . It is danger-ous for a man with a weak heart to go trout-fishing, for he is liable to get a case of shell-shock at any time. You are going down a nice, quiet stream and you see a dark corner over there where a tree hangs out, over a pool which is as smooth as oil and black as ink. You know what is going to happen. You know you're going to be scared. You feel that you shall either jump into the creek or run for home when it does happen. It is manifestly impossible that it should happen at all — and yet that terrifying thing does happen. There comes the tremendous unheralded flash into the air of a crimson and white and orange creature, a terrifying phantasm, a moment seen, then gone forever. Did you see it? Why, yes; but you forgot all about your rod and it certainly must have spit out the fly which it took as it went down half an hour ago. You stand and tremble, and look in apprehension at the spot where the little wrinkles still are spreading out on the oily ink. He might do that again. It takes a brave man to go after trout."

It is surprising how many notables amongst professional workers and men prominent in the larger affairs of business and of the State have succumbed to the allurements of angling. Says Dr. van Dyke: Perhaps the fisherman whom you overtook on the stream " is a man whom you have known in town as a lawyer or a doctor, a merchant or a preacher, going about his business in the hideous respectability of a high silk-hat and a long black coat. How good it is to see him now in the freedom of a flannel shirt and a broad-brimmed grey felt with flies stuck around the band. I have had the good luck to see quite a number of bishops, parochial and diocesan, in that

style, and the vision has always dissolved my doubts
in regard to the validity of their claim to the true
apostolic succession."

The incurable piscatorial proclivities of President
Cleveland and of his eminent surgeon friend Dr.
Bryant, of Joseph Jefferson and of Rev. Dr. van
Dyke himself, are matters of quite common knowledge; but there are many guilty others not known
to the populace. There was Sir Humphry Davy,
Admiral Nelson, Sir Walter Scott, Patrick Henry,
Daniel Webster, " Christopher North " (John Wil-
son, Professor of Moral Philosophy at the University of Edinburgh), Lord Tennyson, Canon Kings-
ley, Audubon the naturalist, James Russell Lowell,
Henry Ward Beecher, President Harrison, Bishop
Potter, and James Whitcomb Riley; and think you
that Thomson, the poet of *The Seasons,* was not a
fisher? Davy tells in his *Salmonia* how, when the
Bishop of Durham inquired of the great Dr. Paley
" when one of his most important works would be
finished, he said, with great simplicity and good
humor, ' My Lord, I shall work steadily at it *when
the fly-fishing season is over.' "* And this reminds
us that Canon Greenwell died in this same Durham
only a year ago the eighteenth of January, at the ripe
age of ninety-seven years. A famous English archæ-
ologist, he was known to the angling world as the
inventor of " Greenwell's Glory," a salmon fly which
has carried his name to rivers in all quarters of the

globe.   The wings of this fly are mottled black and
brown, the legs are made from a red and black
hackle-feather, and the body is dark-brown or olive
silk or wool and ribbed with yellow silk or gold
tinsel.

Continuing with these later days, it would be difficult to cite an example of more capable versatility
than that exhibited in the life of S. Weir Mitchell,
M. D.— equally noted as neurologist and novelist
— and he did not omit a keen enthusiasm for angling.   There is Dr. Richard C. Cabot, who is the
accomplished Assistant Professor of Medicine at
Harvard University and the man responsible for the
modern Social Service hospital idea, whose inspiring
book, *What Men Live By,* should be read and re-
read by everybody, angler or otherwise; and his
confrère at Harvard, Dr. James G. Mumford, author of another charming volume, *A Doctor's Table
Talk.*   The names of the sculptor J. Q. A. Ward, of
" our friend " John Burroughs, of Thomas A. Edi-
son, Eugen Ysaye the great Belgian violinist, Andrew Lang, Viscount Edward Grey, our Secretaries
of State and of the Treasury, Robert Lansing and
William G. McAdoo, the Assistant Secretary of the
Interior, Alexander T. Vogelsang, of Marshal Joffre,
and Sir Harry Lauder, and of a multitude of others
which time and space alone forbid that we should
mention, come to memory; the great surgeon Mc-
Burney, of appendicitis fame, neither do we forget

him, and at the next instant our thoughts instinctively
turn to Dr. Robert T. Morris, who wields a pen as
keen, swift, and sure as his scalpel, when he isn't
wielding the latter, growing nuts, flora- or fauna-
izing, or angling for salmon. As for Andrew Car-
negie, the noted financier and philanthropist, when
at the threshold of his seventies, upon returning from
a brief vacation, he is quoted as having diverted an
interviewer who sought to draw him out concerning
a recent steel operation of magnitude, by exclaiming:
"What is a matter of a few-million dollars' profit
compared with landing a ten-pound pickerel!"
When in his eighties, on July 7th, 1917, angling in
Lake Mahkeenac near Lenox, Mass., he caught two
black bass, thirty-four perch, and ten sunfish, in two-
hours' time, declaring he never enjoyed better sport
on his favorite loch in Scotland; and he was fishing
in these same waters within a few days of his death,
in the Summer of 1919.

The compilation of such a list of memorable men,
of great eminence and learning, who likewise were
great lovers and devotees of angling, has been possible at almost any period in the world's history.
From a famous reference in Father "Iz. Wa." we
will mention "Dr. Nowel, sometimes Dean of S.
Paul's in London (in which Church his Monument
stands yet undefaced) a man that in the Reforma-
tion of Queen Elizabeth was so noted for his meek
spirit, deep Learning, Prudence and Piety, that the

then Parliament and Convocation both, chose, in-
joyned, and trusted him to be the man to make a
Catechism for publick use, such an one as should
stand as a rule for faith and manners to their pos-
teritie: And the good old man (though he was very
learned, yet knowing that God leads us not to
Heaven by many nor by hard questions) like a honest Angler, made that good, plain, unperplext Catechism, that is printed with the old Service Book.   I
say, this good man was as dear a lover, and a con-
stant practicer of Angling, as any Age can produce;
and his custome was to spend (besides his fixt hours
of prayer, those hours which by command of the
Church were enjoined the old Clergy, and voluntarily
dedicated to devotion by many Primitive Chris-
tians:) besides those hours, this good man was observed to spend a tenth part of his time in Angling;
and also (for I have conversed with those which
have conversed with him) to bestow a tenth part
of his Revenue, and usually all his fish, amongst the
poor that inhabited near to those Rivers in which it
was caught, saying often, *That Charity gave life to
Religion:* and at his return to his House would
praise God that he had spent that day free from
worldly trouble, both harmlesly and in a Recreation
that became a Church-man.   And this good man
was well content, if not desirous, that Posterity
should know he was an Angler, as may appear by
his Picture, now to be seen, and carefully kept in

Brazennose College, to which he was a liberal Bene-
factor; in which Picture he is drawn leaning on a
desk with his Bible before him, and on one hand of
him his Lines, Hooks, and other Tackling lying in a
round; and on his other hand are his Angle-rods of
several sorts; and by them this is written, ' That
he died 13 Feb. 1601, being aged 95 years, 44 of
which he had been Dean of St. Paul's Church; and
that his age had neither impaired his hearing, nor
dimmed his eyes, nor weakened his memory, nor
made any of the faculties of his mind weak or use-
less.' 'T is said that Angling and Temperance were
great causes of these blessings, and I wish the like
to all that imitate him, and love the memory of so
good a man."

Continues Walton, " My next and last example
shall be that undervaluer of money, the late Provost
of Eton College, Sir Henry Wotton (a man with
whom I have often fish'd and convers'd) a man
whose foraign imployments in the service of this
Nation, and whose experience, learning, wit, and
cheerfulness, made his company to be esteemed one
of the delights of mankind; this man, whose very
approbation of Angling were sufficient to convince
any modest Censurer of it, was also a most dear
lover, and a frequent practicer of the Art of Angling; of which he would say, ' 'T was an imployment
for his idle time, which was not idly spent;' for Angling was after tedious study, ' A rest to his mind, a

cheerer of his spirits, a diverter of sadness, a calmer of unquiet thoughts, a Moderator of passions, a procurer of contentedness, and that it begat habits of peace and patience in those that profest and practic'd it.'

" Sir, this was the saying of that Learned man; and I do easily believe that peace, and patience, and a calm content did cohabit in the cheerful heart of Sir Henry Wotton, because I know that when he was beyond seventy years of age, he made this description of a part of the present pleasure that possest him, as he sat quietly in a Summer's evening on a bank a fishing; it is a description of the Spring, which because it glided as soft and sweetly from his pen, as that River does now by which it was then made, I shall repeat it unto you:

"This day dame Nature seem'd in love;
The lustie sap began to move;
Fresh juice did stir th' imbracing Vines,
And birds had drawn their Valentines,
The jealous *Trout,* that low did lye,
Rose at a well dissembled flie;
There stood my friend with patient skill,
Attending of his trembling quil.
Already were the eaves possest
With the swift Pilgrim's dawbed nest:
The Groves already did rejoice,
In *Philomel's* triumphing voice:
The showers were short, the weather mild,
The morning fresh, the evening smil'd.
Joan takes her neat rub'd pail, and now
She trips to milk the sand-red Cow;
Where, for some sturdy foot-ball Swain,
Joan strokes a *Sillibub* or twaine;

> The fields and gardens were beset
> With *Tulips, Crocus, Violet,*
> And now, though late, the modest *Rose*
> Did more than half a blush disclose.
> Thus all looks gay, and full of chear
> To welcome the new livery'd year."

Would you go "a-angling" then, thou sedate and solid citizen, be last of all restrained because of the company you will keep. Do you not recall about that historical fishers' lunch around the little camp-fire by the waterside?— "Peter saith, . . . I go a fishing. They say, . . . We also go with thee. . . . Jesus stood on the shore. . . . Then Jesus saith unto them, Children, have ye any meat? They answered him, No. And he said, . . . Cast the net on the right side of the ship, and ye shall find. . . . As soon as they were come to land, they saw a fire of coals there, and fish laid thereon, and bread. Jesus saith, . . . Bring of the fish which ye have now caught. . . . Come and dine. Jesus then cometh, and taketh bread, and giveth them, and fish likewise." If, now, your conservatism still shies at "new-fangled frivolities," read in the nineteenth chapter of Isaiah about "all they that cast angle into the brooks;" in the book of Job, where the Lord asked him, "Canst thou take out a fish with the hook?" or in the first chapter of Habakkuk, how "they take up all of them with the angle."

Perhaps the sustained interest of such men as those referred to is not so surprising either, when we consider the opportunities that angling affords of intimate, leisurely enjoyment of Nature in her most beguiling moods and with the added zest of agreeable companionship; for anglers are admittedly a quiet, considerate, genial, and gentle craft.

The pastime does indeed supply a most happy and inspiring change of activities from the usual more or less sedentary occupations of its most ardent votaries, its varied technic with the combination of open-air life, not too fatiguing exercise, and the complete change of environment being subtly efficacious for the solacement of nerves jangled and out of tune and for the revivifying of the whole man — or woman.   Physicians have reason a-plenty keenly to realize that a warped mentality or a sick soul presents an infinitely more serious problem than does a disordered body.   I have now in mind one who but a few short months ago was the personification of ambition and will power, and who at the present time is a pitiable example of a strong man bereft of confidence and groping and shrinking in the grip of paralyzing fears.   By what means should men strive to forestall such a calamity? and how are they to be helped out of such a Slough of Despond?   Dr. Richard C. Cabot says that what the blind, the worried, the invalid, the discouraged, the convalescent, the neurasthenic, the drug-victim — what the whole world needs both to keep well people well and for the restoration of the sick, is vitality and resisting

power. " As contradistinguished from the hot-
house care of sanitaria, we are realizing more and
more that the sufferer must be encouraged to get
back into real life, which is the best of all teachers
and doctors.   Nothing less fruitful will nourish body
and soul."

   " Real life " he defines as more satisfying and interesting occupation, more recreation or refreshment
through art, play, or natural beauty, deeper and more
intensive affection; and if a fourth resource, worship, gets into life, so much the better, though it has
become today so unfashionable a habit that one
must be prepared to shock the modern ear and to
violate all the scientific proprieties if one confesses
to a belief in it.   The interplay of these four inex-
orable blessings — responsibility, recreation, affection, and through them a glimpse of God — is the
end of life, and the sole worthy end in my creed,
says he; and continues:

   ' I came to the belief first from a doctor's point of
view and as a result of a search for the essential principles of healing within a special field.   This is the
end of all education, all moral training, the food of
the soul in health or in disease, needed by all, to
feed our own souls as well as to cure and to prevent
social ills.   This is the vital nourishment without
which all material relief soon becomes a farce or a
poison, just as medicine in most chronic diseases is a
farce or a poison.   Every human being, man,

woman, and child, hero and convict, neurasthenic and deep-sea fisherman, needs the blessing of God through these four gifts. It is not often, I believe, that a whole life is possessed by any one of the elements of play, work, or drudgery. Work usually makes up the larger part of life, with play and drudgery sprinkled in. I have rarely seen drudgery so overwhelming as to crush out altogether the play of humor and good-fellowship during the day's toil as well as after it.'

So this book has particularly to do with refreshment through the play that is " sprinkled in," through the contact with art — since the building of a bamboo fly-rod and the skilled use thereof both are arts — and with the beauty of nature and its incentive to truest worship of God; and all of this naturally enough is of interest to the medical-man from the viewpoints both of outdoor recreation and of indoor handicraft.

In some way, and at stated intervals, all of us should divert from our routine work, and do something spontaneously — whole-heartedly, with the zest and abandonment of the boy we used to be, and still should be on occasion. For

> " He that works, then runs away,
> Will live to work another day."

Very few of us indeed are so placed as never to find it possible either to " break out " or to " break

away "; none incessantly so situated as was that unknown ancient and most unfortunate author of this
pathetic pair of couplets:

> See I a dog? there 's ne'er a stone to throw!
> Or stone? there 's ne'er a dog to hit I trow!
> Or if at once both stone and dog I view —
> It is the king's dog! Damn! What *can* I do?

Says Dr. A. T. Bristow in *The World's Work*
magazine, " The man who wishes to secure the best
results from the days which he spends in search of
rest and renewed vigor, will not seek the artificial
life of our great hotels with all the attendant excitement, false standards of living, and a table which
is an invitation to gluttony. So we in our struggle
with the gigantic forces which make up modern civil-
ization must return to nature for refreshment and
renewed strength. The forest, the mountains, and
the streams hide the elixir of life. We need to get
away from the crowds, from idle gossip, from the
trivial observances of society, the fetters of custom.
There is no rest like that which is hid for the weary
within the shady recesses of the great woods, and
camp life is far preferable to that counterfeit of
camp life, a hotel in the mountains. You can sleep
as soundly in a bark camp on a thick bed of balsam
as on the softest mattress in a hotel bedroom. A
tramp through the woods is what you need for mind
and body. The fatigue will bring to your tired eyes
sleep far more refreshing than the stuporous slumber

you have experienced in a hotel, superinduced by late hours and the plethora of over-eating without sufficient exercise.

" Remember that there is no better exercise for anyone than walking. It gives the rambler time to learn needed lessons from nature, and it is free from the excitement of high speed, which is the very thing that a vacation should avoid. The man who hurls himself through space in a high-powered automobile is not resting. He simply is substituting one form of mental stimulation for another. He is like those unfortunate victims of the drug habit who go from morphine to cocaine and from both to whisky. Their diseased nerves crave some sort of artificial stimulus. So it often is with our business-men in their ' relaxations.'

" What these men need is the repose of the woods, the calmness of spirit that comes to the tired mind only amidst mountain solitudes. To invite a man of active mind to a ramble through the forest without an incentive is, however, almost as bad as to advise him to saw wood for exercise. Such an occupation affords exercise, but it is a nauseous dose which is too often taken submissively if not with cheerfulness. There is no better motive for the forest wanderer, whether his paths be by mountain stream or highland tarn, than the time-honored sport of good old Izaak Walton. Go a-fishing.

" The angler's art is but a pretext or rather the

"ITS PATRON SAINT IZAAK WALTON"

incentive to a ramble, and not the sole object of the fisherman, unless, alas! he belongs to that too common variety, the man whose sole object is his catch. Such a man fishes always with a worm, hides fingerlings in the depth of his basket, and photographs his catch as a witness to his crimes. He is not a fisherman but a butcher. A yellow primrose on the river's brim is to him a primrose and nothing more. The true fisherman loves to catch fish, to match his wits against the wary trout, but as he wanders from pool to pool the songs of the birds greet him restfully; every turn in the stream reveals a nook in which strange wild flowers nestle. The gentle excitement of the sport prevents the scene from becoming monotonous. The element of chance, the uncertainty of the catch, adds the drop of tabasco sauce which gives zest to the day. And the noontide meal by the brink of the stream! When did a meal have a more delightful flavor? Delmonico never served a trout like unto those we have eaten by the banks of a mountain brook with the clear blue sky above, the waving forest round about and the murmuring stream at our feet. The hour of contemplation comes afterward with the pipe of peace in our hand instead of the relinquished rod. How far off the city seems! Are there such things as corporations, trusts, stocks, bonds; electric lights that amaze the sight, harsh warnings of trolley gongs, the rumble and grind of the wheels and the brakes on the ele-

vated road which affright the ear? The harshest
note that breaks the stillness here is the boom of the
bittern in the distant marsh. Home to camp the
fisherman goes, taking a cast in this silent pool in
which the trout rose in the forenoon to his cast but
missed the fly, or in that dark hole deep under the
bank in which a vigilant eye may detect the brown
sides of a trout with lazily waving fins and tail —
an old campaigner not easily caught.

" So the shades of evening find the ramble ended,
and no harsher beams than the soft radiance of the
stars or the gentle spark of the fireflies and the glow-
worm light the wayfarer to his repose.

" There are other incentives which are able to
make the haunts of wild things attractive. To a
man who has walked through the woods for exercise
much as he would saw wood by a woodpile, a walk
through the tangled paths with a naturalist is both
an astonishment and a revelation. A few years ago
popular works on nature-study were things unknown. The only means of information for the
inquiring amateur were purely technical; works such
as Gray's *Botany,* to a beginner as uninteresting and
difficult as a work on differential calculus. Now there
are whole libraries of books which are both interesting, popular and true to the scientific facts.[2]   There

2 The interested reader will do well to investigate the very inexpensive
Chester A. Reed flower and bird pocket-guides, illustrated in color; Mrs.
Dana's *How to Know the Wild Flowers,* and *How to Know the Ferns;*
the Chapman bird books; Collins and Preston's *Key to the Trees;* Julia
Ellen Roger's *Tree Guide;* Keeler's *Our Native Trees;* F. Schuyler Mathews'

"THE HAUNTS OF WILD THINGS"

are fifty-seven species of fern described in one book, and of these the writer collected twenty-two during a three-weeks' stay in the Adirondacks. Some were found half way up Catamount, some on the slopes of Whiteface, one or two on the face of cliffs overlooking Wilmington. The memories of that Summer are delightful, and as we look over the specimens we gathered in those wanderings, my wife and I, the scenes come back to us and we live those delectable days again."

A long quotation, this, but we freely admit that we could not have said it so well as has Dr. Bristow. We are of those unafraid of quotations, and now invite the reader to attend to this selection from Edwin Sandys, borrowed from the same source as the foregoing. "Fishing leads its devotee into pleasant places, and because the true angler needs must also be part poet, such ears, perhaps, best hear the sermon of streams and stones. There are no cleaner things than pure air and water, and did fishing offer no more than these it would be entitled to consideration. But it does much more, for of it might truly be said: Its ways are pleasant; its paths are peaceful — which means much.

" The more important fishes of our fresh waters, grouped according to habitat, include the salmon, trout, ouananiche, and the grayling, of rapid rivers and brooks and cold lakes of the rock-bound regions;

various field books; etc. Of course he already has made the acquaintance of John Burroughs.

the black, the rock and other basses and the perch of streams and lakes other than typical trout waters; the maskinonge and pike of the Great Lakes and their tributaries, and the various pickerel and the wall-eyed pike common to weedy waters of a great extent of the country.

" Of the salmon and its fishing it is unnecessary to speak at length.   Very few of the salmon rivers of the East are open to the fishing public, and only a specialist with the two-handed tackle is likely to attempt the capture of the king of game-fish.   The ouananiche, too, is not a fish for the masses.   It is a game fighter, and at certain times a free riser, but it is found in but a few of the Northern waters. Its stronghold is Lake St. John, that Mecca of the sportsman northward bound from Quebec City.   In Lake St. John and its tributary rivers, but especially at the lake's outlet, which is the beginning of the famous Saguenay River, is the stronghold of the high-leaping ouananiche, and there the acrobatic small salmon has been taken by many a tourist-angler.   And there are other salmon.   Some of the waters of the Far West at certain seasons are visited by countless salmon of allied yet distinct species, and many a fine fish, though inferior to the Atlantic species, falls victim to the common trolling-spoon and other devices.

" Beyond question the most popular of our game-fish is that spangled aristocrat of the hurrying

stream, the brook-trout.   In addition to his beauty
and palatableness, there is a dash and go about his
method which strongly appeals to those who like
rapid action in their sport — and who does not?
Furthermore, the typical trout water is in itself a
most beautiful thing.   Be the region plain or pictur-
esque, the trout stream surely travels the most attractive part of it.   Follow its musical bickering down a
valley and you will be led through one of Nature's
picture galleries, with choice bits arranged in marvelous profusion upon either side.   Glorious greenery,
lichened rock, grim cliff, echoing vault, thunder-
voiced fall, bubble-spangled ripple and mystic, velvet-
shadowed pool follow in endless succession.   And
with it all the silver song of merry waters, perhaps
chording true at shadowtime with the contralto of
the thrushes.   And so you lose yourself in the en-
chanted cavern of green.

" There is nothing evil to be found in all our hun-
dreds of miles of trout waters.   Only the celestial
pavement itself is cleaner than the pure, sweet water,
forever washing its bed and bounds and forever sing-
ing o'er its wholesome task.   A trout stream is a
good place for most folks to be.   And we have an
abundance of streams — for, broadly speaking, a
rock country is a trout country.   To remove the
trout country from this continent would be to render
it unrecognizable.   There would remain prairies,
marshlands, the regions of sluggish streams and

placid ponds. The best of the easily reached free
fishing is to be enjoyed upon the hill streams of the
Adirondacks, Pennsylvania, and Connecticut. If
you go farther there are still within reasonable distance the famous waters of the Rangeley and Moose-
head systems of Maine, the Megantic waters of Quebec, the wilds of New Brunswick, the marvelous
silver net of the North shore of the St. Lawrence and
of Northern Ontario, which extends to the newly
exploited region of the upper Ottawa and to that
stronghold of big trout, the North shore of Lake
Superior. All of these regions, both American and
Canadian, are comfortably accessible by rail, and no
railroad worthy of the name fails to pay strict attention to the comfort of anglers.

"I have fished in every one of the extensive regions named, and the average angler may visit any
one of them with a certainty of enjoying fair fun
and an excellent chance of extraordinary sport.
Were the purse, leisure, and experience, or lack of it,
of every reader known, it would be a comparatively
easy task to name one particular water which would
be almost certain to meet the requirements; but
lacking full knowledge of individual desires, any
attempt at the rôle of guide-post would be absurd.
But the individual can get helpful, because as a whole
reliable, information by securing a sporting guide-
book of a rail-road traversing the preferred country. Because I have written some of them and read

the others I know they are not dangerously enthusiastic, especially over the more remote waters.
In fact, not a few of them actually fail to do full
justice to the regions they refer to. The pen of a
wizard of word-painting could not overdraw the
beauties of at least four-fifths of our trout waters,
which will, under ordinary conditions, yield all the
fish that clean sportsmanship can demand."

Very true, Mr. Sandys — and also true that good
sport, if not the most exciting, may be reached from
most of the humble homes of the land, within a reasonable journey for the ubiquitous Ford, the motor-
cycle, bicycle, trolley-car, or even shanks' mare.
There are the Sullivan County and other Catskill
streams of New York, streams of the White Mountain region in New Hampshire, streams in Vermont,
New Jersey, and in Massachusetts. We have seen a
dozen native trout creeled legitimately in August,
only three days before the close of the season, from
public water not fifteen miles out of New York City.
And almost any pond will yield either bass, pickerel,
or such very acceptable pan-fish as perch, rock-bass,
or " sunnies."

With a similar charming felicity have many other
writers depicted the joys of angling. Of the numerous pleasures that are closely connected with its pur-
suit —" its accompaniments and variations, which
run along with the tune and weave an embroidery of
delight around it," to borrow a fragment of Dr. van

Dyke's plenitude of happy phraseology — the intimate study of stream insect-life and the pretty art
of the tying of artificial flies in imitation of these
ephemera, in particular, constitute a very soul-satis-
fying diversion and accomplishment.   But having
already discussed this elsewhere, it is the writer's
present paramount purpose to enlighten those who
would add to their accustomed enjoyment of the
sport the pleasures of craftsmanship involved in the
construction of the angler's chief implement of his
art, that magic wand, his *rod*.

When touching upon this phase of the subject even
a professional rod-maker needs must lean to poesy
in order to explain adequately why the rod plays the
most important part in the angler's equipment, as
witness this extract from a trade catalog: " Its development to the present state of perfection has
heightened the enjoyment of the sport to a degree
far beyond any that was attainable by the angler of
the olden time.   The ecstatic period of supreme sen-
sation which is peculiarly the angler's inspiration and
delight was formerly of short duration, and often
with inglorious ending.   Not so today, for the modern rod has made it possible for the entrancing thrill
that comes to him through the titillation of the elbow
by the vibratory connection of his hand and arm with
a gamy fish at the other end of a rod and line, to be
long drawn out, with intensely stimulating variations,
in a contest calling into play the highest qualities of

manly sportsmanship, and in which both victor and
vanquished may fairly be credited with honors nobly
won." Is any further assurance needed that this
man makes good rods? Anyway, we will say right
here that he does — beauties.

The acme of perfection in angling-rods —" the
rod fine-tempered with elastic spring "— is realized
only in one built properly of six strips of split bamboo. In the maximum combination of the qualities
of resiliency, balance, and lightness with power,
quickness, and smoothness or sweetness of action,
such an one is unsurpassed; and the split-bamboo rod
of the best American manufacture has no superior
the world over. In making this statement we are
not heedless of the improvements upon this standard
model that have been attempted, principally by our
English cousins across the big pond. Various pain-
fully ingenious combinations have been achieved, of
bamboo without and steel core within, steel core
within and braided steel, copper, or bronze ribbands
outside, split cane inside and whole cane outside, and
all sorts of other arrangements, in eight strips of
cane, in nine strips, built double in twelve, sixteen,
or eighteen strips — modifications leading all the
way up — or down — to the rolled tubular whole-
steel rod of American make. Most of these variations are possible only for the butt- and middle-
joints of a rod, the top-joint or top — or as American anglers say less explicitly, the tip — being gen-

erally of clear bamboo. The British manufacturer has a penchant also for combining different woods in individual rods, as a greenheart butt- and second-joint with a bamboo top, or an ash or hickory butt with greenheart and bamboo for the other sections.

But of any of these mongrels we will have naught; as for us we pin our faith and fealty to the silk-wound hexagonal rod cunningly yet simply devised of its six subtle, individual triangular strips of cane throughout, and we can but view with compassion that angler who suffers a permanent perverted attachment to some one or other of the monstrosities mentioned above.

The making of a split-bamboo rod is readily within the accomplishment of anyone who can handle a few of the simpler carpenters'-tools, with patience — and your true angler already has this quality well developed. A little time, a little absorbingly interesting work, a small outlay for rod fittings or mountings, and forty-cents' worth of bamboo in the rough is transformed into the most beautiful of all sporting implements, that the owner could not have duplicated by a professional rod-maker for forty dollars. A knife, a small plane, and a file are the principal necessary cutting tools, and with two or three simple contrivances, and one all-important device, these cover the essential instruments.

Almost any manual labor, especially if diverting and concentrating the attention into novel paths, is balm for the jaded or worried mind. This work is light and innately fascinating. How it would have been welcomed by many persons whom the writer has known, while monotonously convalescent from exasperating illness or accident; how it would have sweetened and shortened the days and have proven hypnotic at night for many a weary traveler along the road to restored bodily health and mental serenity. Patients often read and read during a forced period of shutting-in until they can't read any longer, and don't know what in the world next to do to alleviate the tedium of the dragging hours and days. We escaped this experience during an eight-weeks' quarantine for scarlet fever, in beguiling many an hour by winding rod-joints with silk, satisfied that the subsequent coats of varnish preceded by an alcohol bath would prove effectively disinfectant. It was during this incarceration that first we learned of the virtues of pinochle; and the feeling nightly adieu of our teacher Jones, repeated each day with increasing unction, comes back to us as we write these words — the place was the City Hospital: " Thank God! one more day less in the pest-house."

Not only is the angler's sport, like any other, greatly enhanced by the employment of implements of his own creation, but the very making of a rod is an idyl in craftsmanship, furnishing a recreation salutary and delightful in itself during the wintry days which debar actual but not anticipatory enjoyment of limpid lakes, quiet woodland trails, inspiring mountain heights, merry brooks, and companionable little rivers.

After experiencing for many years the pleasures to be derived from the possession of this handicraft, and having gained from that experience, including conference with brother anglers addicted to the same avocation, the most vital parts of what he knows about the subject, it becomes an added pleasure for the writer to pass the knowledge along to yet other Waltonians, who hitherto have missed this culminating enjoyment of their favorite sport. Thus, as truly as did " Piscator " in the writing of his immortal pastoral, the present author likewise has " made a recreation of a recreation "; and too has endeavored, despite its technical character, to have his text " not to read dully and tediously."

The reader is assured at the outset that by careful attention to and the following out of the very explicit directions contained in the chapters immediately following, he can construct not merely a passably-good split-bamboo rod, but a high-grade article that any expert angler would be glad to own — a rod that will have balance, action, finish, and distinction, and the possession of which will give infinite satisfaction to its creator. Admittedly, the process involves some manipulations of delicacy but none of discouraging difficulty, as all there is to it may be

"QUIET WOODLAND TRAILS"

(An Adirondack carry)

summed up in careful attention to a number of details in their proper sequence and not one of which truly is difficult in itself — and what could be better exercise for youth? for the same constitutes the successful conduct of life. From the standpoint of commercial manufacture, while some of the ways and means which will be elucidated might provoke a smile from the professional rod-maker — and we will not say without justification — nevertheless they will be found fully efficient for the production of one or two to a dozen or more rods for the personal equipment of the amateur angler, to whom our remarks are addressed.   So —

Here's to the swish of the Split-Bamboo! —
Flitting my flies o'er riffle and pool,
Bidding all grown-up cares adieu,
Back again coming to Nature's school,
May the wind blow soft, my cast light true,
As *Fontinalis* I try to fool,
And my creel have received its due
When come the shades of evening cool.—
Here's to the swish of the Split-Bamboo! —
Musical swish of *my own* bamboo.

ROD-MAKING:

BAMBOO AS A ROD MATERIAL

CHAPTER II

ROD-MAKING:
BAMBOO AS A ROD MATERIAL

The material of which split-bamboo angling-rods of quality are made is not derived from our American Southern species, inferior in strength and elasticity, but chiefly is bamboo from India or the Tonkin (Tonquin) cane from the province of that name, which is the most northerly one of Cochin China. Though differing in features to be noted, both of these grow under similar climatic conditions. We have no personal acquaintance with Japanese cane.

Bamboo or *Bambusa* is a genus of grasses, of approximately one-hundred species, attaining a height generally of from twenty to one-hundred feet. They all have an underground root-stock which throws up from five to one-hundred stems. The straight horizontal branches are not developed until the stems have reached their full height and they are denser toward the top. The stems or stalks (botanically, " culms ") are jointed, like those of other grasses, and contain within only a light, spongy pith except at the joints or nodes, where they are divided by strong partitions. Upon the outside of the stalks are circumscribing ridges corresponding to the site of the partitions within. Because of

these partitions, sections of bamboo-stalk are readily converted into water-bottles, and, upon removal of the partitions, the stalks of the larger species, attaining a diameter of five or six inches, are used in the Orient for piping water.

Interest attaches to the use of the word " cane " as applied to bamboo. Botanically, cane refers to any plant having long, hard,

Growing bamboo

elastic stems. Walking-sticks originally were designated " canes " only when made of cane, as from the smaller stems of bamboo imported into Europe for this purpose. Thus bamboo does not derive its name of cane from the walking-stick, but, conversely, " cane " as applied generally to the walking-stick arose from the specific use of cane in the manufacture thereof.

Bamboo-stalk is remarkable for its combined hardness, strength, lightness, and elasticity, and these qualities, together with its availability and the ease with which it may be split into narrow strips, at once commend it for a multitude of uses, such as for mats, baskets, pipe-stems, spear and lance shafts, flutes, palaquin-poles, masts, for building furniture, houses, and bridges.

In all species the outer covering of the stem is extremely hard and siliceous, and its walls become progressively softer and more friable from without toward the inner pith. The knots of some species of bamboo exude a sweetish juice which exposure to the air thickens into a gum that the Greeks called " Indian honey." The fruit of some varieties is a grain, of others a nut, or again a fleshy product more like an apple. Some young bamboo-shoots are eaten like asparagus with us.

As has been said, bamboo grows in all sizes, from the species attaining only a few feet in height to the *Bambusa Guadua* of New Granada or the Java article, which may have trunks sixteen inches in diameter; and the stems of the different species vary much in the thickness of the woody part. A smoothly cut cross-section of the stalk will show its walls to be cellular or honeycombed in character, the cells being more closely compacted as the outer

surface is approached. The depth of this
" enamel " or strength-imparting stratum varies both
actually and relatively to the thickness of individual
stem-walls; and different species of bamboo, as also
different stems of the same species, vary considerably
in their straightness of growth.   In all species the
rate of growth is very rapid and in some almost in-
credibly so.

It goes without saying that stems having relatively thicker and denser enamel strata will be superior for use where strength and elasticity are prime
requisites; and this factor of hardness or solidity together with straightness of the stems and knots that

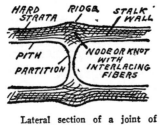

are but slightly swollen,
is what particularly com-
mends bamboo for rod-
making.

Upon bending a strip
split from a bamboo-stem,
the convexity of the curve
corresponding to the outer

Lateral section of a joint of
bamboo stalk through node

or " rind " side, when the breaking-point is reached
it will be noted that this hard outer layer is composed of long fibers which splinter into brush-
like ends.   These fibers are interrupted at the nodes
or knots and interlace there, and when the strength-
ening partition is cut away they mark the weakest
place in the wall; a strip will easily *break off short
at this point.*

Up to some thirty-odd years ago most manufac-
turers of angling-rods employed the Indian (Calcutta) bamboo for their purpose, and an occasional
veteran angler will be encountered today who firmly
believes that a Calcutta-bamboo rod is the only bamboo rod.   But the truth of the matter is that the
day of the Calcutta rod has passed; and yet the best
rods made now are far better than any that Dad or
even Grandfather ever owned.   A conspicuous superficial feature identifying the Indian cane is the
irregularly mottled effect produced by the burn- or
scorch-marks, always found on this variety and contrasting prettily with its naturally yellow rind when
thoroughly seasoned.   This ordinarily is not seen in
the Tonkin or Chinese cane, and when found in the
experience of the author it was neither so extensive
nor fantastic.   The latter bamboo, as purchased in
the American market, generally has a smooth un-
marked surface of a little brighter yellow shade than
that of the Calcutta cane.

Encyclopedia references make no note of these artificial brown markings which ordinarily are taken
to be merely decorative.   Henry P. Wells mentions
six possible explanations of their occurrence in his
Fly-Rods and Fly-Tackle.   To the best knowledge
of the present writer they are the result of searing
the green bamboo-stalks with hot irons in the drying
out and straightening process, before marketing
them.

As the first split-bamboo rods offered the angling fraternity were made of the Calcutta cane, it was natural that these markings came to be indissolubly associated with the only genuine thing in such rods. Later on, when for one reason or another it became increasingly difficult to secure a high grade of Calcutta bamboo for the American rod-maker, recourse was had to the Tonkin variety, and today by far most of the best rods both of domestic and British manufacture — and including the two brands most generally regarded as the best of all — are made of the Tonkin cane.

Very likely the reason for the usual absence of scorch-marks on Tonkin bamboo is that its stalks grow straighter than those of the Calcutta article, thus making it of less importance to " take out the kinks " before sending it to market.   However, for the purpose of rod-making, it doubtless was expedient for a time to reproduce on the Tonkin cane marks similar to those which had become familiar to persons acquainted with the Calcutta bamboo, and intimately associated in their minds with the intrinsic qualities of elasticity, etc., highly desirable in an angling-rod.   To this end some strongly-corrosive acid may have been employed at times.   But when the Tonkin article came to be fully proven the equal of if not superior to the other for this specific purpose, then the trade could afford to put it into rods

undisguised and unadorned, strictly on its own un-
deniable merits.

Most of the bamboo that reaches America comes
in as ballast for returning light cargoes, and as purchased from the dealer the tyro rod-maker will receive it in butts or stalks of from four to six feet in
length. The six-foot " sticks " are what he preferably should ask for; and they will vary in diameter,
at the larger end, from a little more than one inch
to two inches; they will average about an inch-and-a-
quarter, and have a maximum thickness of wall of
from three-sixteenths to three-eighths of an inch.
For some reason — apparently mysterious because
of the prevalence and rapid growth of bamboo and
the size attained by many varieties — larger butts
are not obtainable in the American market. Our
own impression is that this may be explained by the
fact that these readily obtainable larger kinds are
of more rapid growth, of looser fiber, and deficient
in elasticity; and experience would seem to have con-
firmed this. Through an interested friend in touch
with an Oriental importing-house, and after months
of correspondence — starting in India with officials
at the Calcutta Botanical Gardens — we received
some stalks over ten feet long, very smooth and
straight, nearly three inches in diameter, and measuring over three feet between knots; but the stuff was
thin-walled and deficient in hardness, compactness of

fiber, and elasticity, like our native bamboo. It would make beautiful *cases* for rods, however. It may be, too, that bamboo from a locality which exposes the growing stalks to frequent bending in the wind will develop superior elasticity; and strips from the side of an individual stalk that was most exposed to the weather may have a preferable steely quality.

Of the numerous varieties of the Indian bamboo, it would appear that the particular one known botanically as *Dendrocalamus strictus* would be the best for rod-making, though it has been stated that the *Bambusa arundinacea* is the Calcutta cane often used for the purpose. The former is described as follows, by J. S. Gamble, in an article on the *Bambuseæ of British India,* Annals of the Calcutta Botanical Gardens, vol. 7, p. 79. We quote directly from a pamphlet issued by the U. S. Department of Agriculture, captioned: " Seeds from a Bamboo from Calcutta, India, presented by Mr. William Bambower, Collins, Ohio "—

A very useful and strong bamboo of India, formerly used universally for spear shafts. The plant flowers frequently and does not die down after flowering as in the case with so many bamboos. The culms are said to sometimes reach a height of one-hundred feet. This is the most common and most widely spread and most universally used of the Indian bamboos, and is commonly known as the "male" bamboo. Its culms are employed by the natives for all purposes of building and furniture, for mats, baskets, sticks, and other purposes. It furnishes, when large culms are procurable, the best material for lance shafts. In Burma, when large culms are obtainable, they are much in request for mats [masts?] for native boats. It flowers gregariously over large areas, as it did in the Central Provinces in 1865, but it may be found flowering sporadically, a few clumps at a time almost every year, in any locality, and such clumps then usually die off. These flowerings, however, do not produce as much good seed as when the gregarious flowering takes place. The flowers appear in the cold season between November and April, the seed ripening in June. The leaves fall in February or March, and the young new ones appear in April. The young culms are rather late, usually beginning to appear in July sometime after the rains begin.

As compared with the Calcutta bamboo, the rind or compact enamel, outside layer of Tonkin cane is thicker and harder, the " wood " cuts yellower — not unlike a piece of miniature yellow pine — its fibers are coarser, and strips split from it have a stiffer elasticity.   Of two rods of equal dimensions, that made of Calcutta cane will be a bit lighter in weight and more pliant — will have less " backbone."   In two other respects the Calcutta is easier to work: its softer, whiter fiber planes easier where the Tonkin requires more frequent sharpenings of the planing-iron, and the fibers also being finer (it makes a more hair-like brush on breaking) and less cohesive, it splits both truer and more readily.   In two more-important respects the Tonkin cane is pleasanter to work: it is straighter, deflecting less from node to node; and the nodes themselves — both the partitions inside and the corresponding circular ridges outside — are much less prominent and so less distorting to the symmetry of the stick and of strips split therefrom.   Also, in this variety, depressions at the ridges, marking the site where fronds or leaves have dropped or been cut away, are rarely noticeable in the butts delivered by the bamboo dealer, whereas in the Calcutta sticks they always are found — and in an aggravated form due to the leaf being set deeper into the stalk — and render it impossible to utilize in rod-making longitudinal strips split from their entire circumference. In other words, much of the Calcutta-bamboo stalk must be counted as waste material in building rods.

In selecting bamboo butts, pick out those having a decidedly well-seasoned, clear yellow appearance rather than a greenish tinge, reject any showing burn-marks penetrating deeply into the fiber of the wall, and, other things being equal — as degree of seasoning, especially — size for size, a stick having denser and thicker enamel will weigh heavier. Grayish stains may be the result of mildew. Well-seasoned hard-fibered stock will give out a clear ring when struck with a stick, quite different from the flat sound of green cane.

Some fishing-tackle dealers have been reluctant in the past to supply stick bamboo to amateur rod-builders, but during more recent years many of them have very sensibly pursued a more farsighted policy. The writer has obtained perfectly satisfactory sound and well-seasoned Tonkin-bamboo butts from the Robert Ogilvie Company, 79 Chambers Street, New York City; J. Deltour, 1112 Forest Avenue, Bronx, New York City; the Fred D. Divine Company,

Utica, N. Y.; James Heddon's Sons, Dowagiac, Mich.; and the T. H. Chubb Rod Company, Post Mills, Vt. From Abbey and Imbrie, 97 Chambers Street, New York City, he has procured both Tonkin and Calcutta cane. The average cost for six-foot sticks was about forty cents each.

We will add that prominent dealers in anglers' supplies carry in stock split-bamboo rod-joints, *glued up but unmounted, unwound, and unvarnished,* for those who wish to repair or assemble rods, but who may hesitate to undertake the more complex work of actually building joints. The cost of the first-quality machine-made article of this description is about one dollar per joint; for handmade, from two to three dollars. The writer began his rod work by assembling, mounting, winding, and finishing such glued-up stock. In some cases it may be advisable to start in the game after this fashion, but the resultant satisfaction is not comparable with that experienced by the angler who is the fond possessor of a set of rods which represents his own thought and handiwork from start to finish, which he knows absolutely to be composed throughout the entire length of each and every section of solid, tough fiber clear to the center, and who is independent of outside assistance in making repairs, even to the extent of constructing new joints to replace such as may have suffered smash-ups.

We regret to have to state that we have seen in

one of the oldest and most reliable anglers' outfitting-shops, one of the most famous makes of bamboo rod, that had at one point in its circumference *four knots in line* out of the six strip-sections. The price of that rod was thirty-five dollars. The novice will better appreciate the significance of this statement when he reads the ensuing chapter. Also, we have a friend who, accidentally smashing a joint of his "classy" split-bamboo, decided to take advantage of this opportunity to investigate and see just what value he had obtained for his thirty-odd dollars. Cross-sections of the joint at various points revealed a hole running through its center that would almost admit a steel knitting-needle. We fear that in some instances, with better facilities for manufacturing and with increased output, the American handmade split-bamboo has been bereft of intimate personal solicitude in the making, and in consequence has deteriorated in that quality which once made the name invariably synonymous with " the best in the world."

ROD-MAKING:

SPLITTING OUT, STRAIGHTENING, AND ASSEMBLING THE STRIPS

CHAPTER III

ROD-MAKING:
SPLITTING OUT, STRAIGHTENING,
AND ASSEMBLING THE STRIPS

That genius surely had an inspiration who first conceived the idea of constructing an angling-rod hexagonally, in longitudinal sections composed of glued and silken-bound triangular strips of the strongest, outer part only of the walls of bamboo-cane, thus achieving straight and practically solid joints, equally elastic and resistant in all directions, and of a hitherto unheard-of strength in comparison with their delicate caliber and astonishingly light weight. Kit Clarke, noted veteran angler and author of *Where the Wild Trout Hide,* and who died only recently, in his eighty-fifth year, credits the invention to Sam Phillipi, a gunmaker of Easton, Pa., about the year 1862.

But while the standard split-bamboo, as now known, is probably of American origin, the credit for the first rods made of actual rent cane-strips we have to admit belongs to England.[3] The Phillipi rod-

[3] For the following data concerning the history of the " split-bamboo " we are indebted to articles by Messrs. William Mitchell and Lawrence D.

joints were made in three longitudinal sections. About 1860, E. A. Green of Newark, N. J., made up for the trade a few rods in four longitudinal sections, followed in 1863 or 1864 by an acquaintance, a Mr. Murphy, also of Newark. Thaddeus Norris used one of these Phillipi, Green, or Murphy rods. The first rods in *six* bamboo sections were put on the American market by H. L. Leonard of Bangor, Me., about 1870, though Mr. Murphy claimed to have made one some time previously.

William Mitchell says the first split-bamboo he ever saw or heard of was made by William Blacker, of 54, Dean Street, Soho, London, to order for Mr. James Stevens, the well-known sportsman of Hoboken, N. J., and that in 1852 it was given to him for repairs and alterations. Blacker was the author of *Fly Making and Angling*, London, 1855, and he says on page 82: "The rent and glued-up bamboo-cane rods, which I turn out to the greatest perfection [and thus we see where all the modern makers obtained their literary cue], are very valuable, as they are very light and powerful, and throw the line with great facility."

Thomas Aldred, of London, claimed to be the inventor of the three-section or -strip glued-up bamboo rod, at some date prior to the Crystal Palace

Alexander, appearing in vol. II of *Sport with Gun and Rod*, published by The Century Co., in 1883, though their original source is *The American Angler*. Mr. Mitchell himself first made a split-cane rod, in four longitudinal sections of Chinese bamboo, "which is much harder and more homogeneous," in June, 1869.

Exhibition, in 1851, at which Ainge and Aldred, J. Bernard, and J. K. Farlow exhibited the implement. The Aldred firm showed their rod also at the Exhibition in 1853, at New York. All these rods were of three longitudinal sections, running the whole length of the cane, and not in strips glued up with staggered knots. In 1856 there was printed in London an edition of Walton's *Compleat Angler*, with notes on fishing-tackle by the publisher, Henry C. Bohn. On page 325 he says: "The split or glued-up rod is difficult to make well, and very expensive. It is made of three pieces of split cane, which some say should have the bark inside, some outside, nicely rounded."

In the first edition of his *Handbook of Angling*, London, 1847, Edward Fitzgibbon quotes Mr. Little, of 15, Fetter Lane, rod-maker to His Royal Highness Prince Albert, and speaking of the top- and middle-joints of a salmon rod, as follows: "They are to be made from the stoutest pieces of bamboo-cane, called 'jungle,' and brought from India. The pieces should be large and straight, so that you can rend them well through knots and all. Each joint should consist of three rent pieces, . . . and afterward glued together, knot opposite to knot . . but the best part opposite to that which may be imperfect, so as to equalize defectiveness and goodness. The natural badness of the cane you counteract by art, and none save a clever workman can do it. . . . If the pieces are skilfully glued together, they will require no redressing, except at the corners, to bring the rod from the three-square to the round shape.   I am prepared to prove that there are not more than three men in London capable of making, perfectly, rods of solid cane, rent, glued, and then correctly finished with the bark lying on the outside." Mr. Fitzgibbon himself adds: " In my opinion, rods . . . made entirely of rent and glued jungle-cane are the best.   They must be most carefully fashioned, and no maker can turn them out without charging a high price.   I am also of opinion that they will last longer than any other sort of rod, and are far less liable to warping.   I have a high opinion of their elasticity, and Mr. Bowness, fishing-tackle maker of No. 12, Bellyard, Temple Bar, showed me once a trout fly-rod, made in this, my favorite way, *that had been for many years in use* and was still straight as a wand.   I never saw a better single-handed rod."   After this discerning comment, it arouses one's curiosity to note that in the second edition of his book, published only a year later (1848), " Ephemera " writes: " I have changed my opinion with respect to rods made entirely of rent cane or any other wood rent.   Their defects will always more than counterbalance their merits."

Allowing therefore a reasonable interpretation to the expression " for many years," this would seem to show indisputably that rods of " rent jungle-cane " were made as far back as 1830–40.

The accompanying cross-section diagrams will at once make clear exactly what part of the bamboo-stick is used, and how the strips so split out and cut down to form are combined in the completed individual joints or sections of a modern rod.

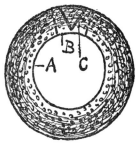

A — Cross-section of bamboo stalk
B — Rough-split rectangular strip
C — Split strip planed to triangular form

It is to be understood that each individual strip of a joint is in cross-section an equilateral triangle, except for the slight convexity of its outer surface which remains un-touched by the cutting-tool; that each strip has a

Cross-section of com-pleted (glued) rod-joint

definite taper from its butt to the top end; and that each joint throughout the whole symmetrically-tapered rod, from the rod's butt of one-half inch, more or less, in diameter to its delicate tip of a scant one-sixteenth inch or little more in thickness, is composed of six of these exactly similar strips. The uninitiated on being shown, with this explanation, the top-joint of an eight- to nine-foot fly-rod weighing, complete, from four to five ounces, and easily capable of bringing to the landing-net a five-pound streak of lightning scientifically designated *Salvelinus fontinalis,* are very likely to be incited to that somewhat trite though unctiously satisfactory retort, "You 're a liar!" Yet 't is even so. And now it becomes the writer's great pleasure to descend to brass tacks and explain in detail how this miracle is wrought.

Having acquired his cherished sticks from the nearest available source, the prospective engineer and constructer conveys them homeward with a palpitating heart. Other tremors of that same cardiac organ are due to occur ere his delightful and fearsome task is completed. True to advice, he has selected well-seasoned stock having a good depth of enamel, but he will see to it that his material has further opportunity to ripen well before he makes use of the completed rod. To this end he will begin immediately by splitting his sticks lengthwise into quarters, thus breaking through all partitions at the nodes and admitting the air freely to the pith side of the bamboo tube. Remember this is Winter, and that many weeks are to elapse before the advent of the blithesome Springtime — so there is no hurry. Do not start this job if you are obsessed with any idea of haste. Not that after a short time you will be unable to turn out rods with a very respectable alacrity; but do not fail to *begin* under the beneficent influence of the feeling of abundant leisure for your project.

After the sticks have been quartered you may proceed to split out rectangular strips roughly approximating the final size required for use in individual joints. These also may stand aside in a dry place, and *season some more.* The degree of seasoning and elasticity may be tested by bending a slender piece sharply between the hands and noting how quickly and completely it regains its former lines upon releasing one end. You also may test the surplus ends of strips, in selecting those for use, by bending them until they break. The harder it is to break them and the longer the splintering fracture, the better the material is suited to your purpose. Then, after planing the strips down to final dimensions and collating them into their respective joints, temporarily bound with coarse thread, they may well *season some more.* After the joints are glued up they will not be hurt by a little more laying aside and additional seasoning before varnishing; and after the rod has received its last finishing-touches, is jointed and hung up by its tip — well, it really is all the better if it be let hang to *season some more,* before putting it to use.

Professional makers prefer that a finished high-grade rod shall have several months' rest before reaching the hands of the angler, and some even allow their glued-up joints to season a whole year before assembling and mounting them into rods.

But now to our mutton, that is, our splitting. To be sure, splitting is splitting, planing is planing, gluing is gluing, winding is winding, and varnishing is varnishing; but most emphatically there are ways, and other ways, of attempting each and all of these things — do we not know it! If desirous of getting into trouble " right off the reel," take an ordinary jack-knife and a quarter-section of Tonkin cane and, drawing toward you, just split off nicely and evenly say a three-eighths-inch approximately rectangular strip from its edge — just " free and easy like." Try it and see whère you arrive.

But bamboo, either Calcutta or Tonkin, may be split very easily and true, and here is the way to do it. If the reader can improve upon the method or any of the other technic carefully detailed in this book, as *later* he may, well and good; but take the advice that for the *beginner in split-bamboo rod-building,* implicit conformity to the instructions of one who has been there spells immunity from the devil of discouragement and failure and hence is altogether the better part of valor. This dose of preventive medicine should suffice.

Procure from the hardware store a solid-blade better grade knife of the kitchen utility style. The illustration conveys the idea, and the cost will be twenty-five or thirty cents; or a cheap steel-blade table-knife, such as you find in the ten-cent stores, will serve. With the butt-end of the bamboo-stick on the floor — and yourself mounted on a chair or a box — place the knife-blade across the middle of

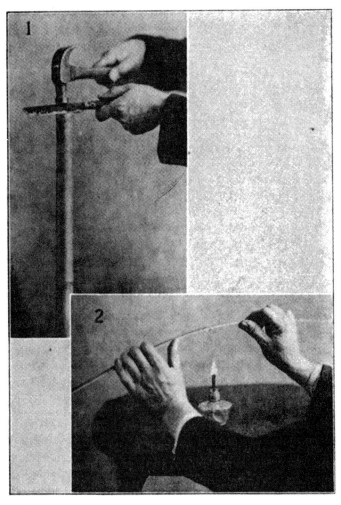

1—Halving stalks 2—Corrective bending over alcohol lamp

the upper end and hit it squarely with a hammer, splitting the cane in halves down to the first node. Now push the knife down into contact with the partition at this node and with a similar blow cut through that. Next, seize each split-off half-portion between thumb and finger and pull them apart. This will split the stick evenly down to the second node. Cut through this as before, again pull the halves apart, and so continue until the whole length of the cane is divided. With Calcutta bamboo, halve it through the depressions where the leaves were attached, which are on opposite sides at alternate nodes.

The same operation repeated will divide your halves evenly into quarters, when you now set about removing the outside ridges and the parts of the partitions from the strips. For the ridges, the effective tool is a medium-coarse *cross-hatched* file (not a mill-saw file, which will not take hold) ; and

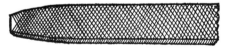

Cross-hatched file

you should file straight across, at right-angles to the strip (not draw-filing, sideways), which is conveniently held for the purpose, convex side up, between the jaws of an iron vise. Having filed all the ridges level with the surface of the adjacent wood, you now may place your quarter-section strips concave or pith side up in the vise, to remove the partitions with gouge and hammer, flush with the inner surface. The strips will now appear as shown.

Another effective way of breaking the halves into quarters, is first to remove the ridges and partitions, then to place the pieces between the vise-jaws, horizontally on the flat, and screw up the vise till the bamboo cracks.

Of course the worker must have a workbench, which need not be over six-feet long, with a level top not less than fifteen-inches wide, and it is important that it be so situated that operations may be conducted in a good light; and as to the vise, he will find that one of cast-steel, with four-inch jaws having hardened faces, will serve nicely, as well as for all other purposes of household carpentry and repairing. (Don't suppose for a moment that you are going to manufacture " fishing-poles " in the house with impunity and balk at mending a broken chair, or at some other little odd-job that wifey jogs you about.) Such a vise will cost from three to four dollars as against the six or eight dollars asked for one of forged steel; and it will fulfill all the functions of the more expensive tool excepting for such heroic work as bending a stiff piece of iron held in the jaws, by striking it against the side with a heavy hammer.

Our quarter-sections of cane are now ready for

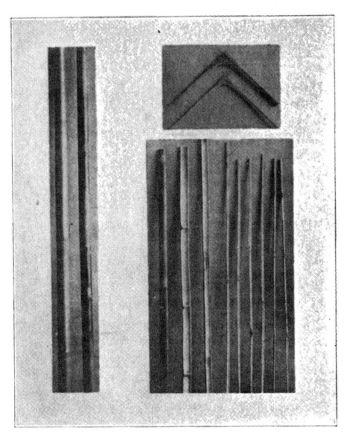

Tonkin and Calcutta bamboo stalks (at left)

Splintered strips of Tonkin and Calcutta cane (top)

Outside of section of stalk with ridges filed away; inside of
  section showing remains of partitions; same with partitions cut away; and six narrow rent strips (lower right)

further splitting into approximately square or rectangular strips *just a bit thicker* than actually needed just before trimming them down to their final form, ready for gluing up into rod-joints.

We go about this second splitting somewhat differently. The section to be split into these narrower strips is laid upon its back, convex side against the bench. The knife now is held with its length lengthwise of the strip, the point of the blade being placed against the inner surface at the knots or remains of the nodes, as it receives the blow of the hammer. Thus we now are splitting on the flat, from within outward, and not endwise of the wood as before. Begin at the top and split successively at each knot, moving toward the bottom end of the strip. After the hammer-blow has sunk the knife-blade through the knot, give the knife a sudden side-prying wrench, which extends the split for some distance both ways from the knot. When all the knots have thus been split through, take hold of the top of the narrow strip to be rent off and complete its separation by smartly pulling it away.

In assembling the strips to be used in individual rod-joints,[4] it is necessary that most of them be cut *some inches longer than the intended length of the completed joint*, for the reason that some of the bamboo necessarily is sacrificed in the next process,

4 The word "joint" may signify either an individual rod-section, the ferrule connection, the knot at site of a node in the bamboo, or the node itself.

which is known as " slipping the joints " or knots.
This means simply that at no circumference of the
completed joint should knots be found opposite to
each other; thus every weak spot, as indicated by the
situation of a knot, is supported by solid, long-fibered
enamel all the way around the remainder of the rod
at this point.   This staggered construction is the
American usual and preferable practise, although we
know of one of the most famed of British makers
who systematically puts three knots in line but on
alternate faces of his joints.   Probably he thinks
that a more subtly harmonious action of the rod
is thereby achieved.

The arrangement of the six narrow strips of a
prospective joint, properly assembled preparatory to
being trimmed to length, will be something like that
shown in the illustration.   Insomuch as these nodes,

Slipping or staggering the knots

in bamboo are situated varying distances apart, and
even in the individual stems — they are closer toward the butt end of the cane — two strips split
from parallel parts of one stalk, and one being
turned end for end and thus laid up against its mate,
will have their knots mismatched or staggered; and

without demanding here any sacrifice of bamboo in order to accomplish this result, so far as the relation, one to the other, of just these two individual strips is concerned.

The concave or pith surface of each strip is now planed *just sufficiently to flatten them,* after which their sides are planed only enough to make them smooth.   For all planing, the five-and-one-half inch " Stanley " iron-plane, number 103, and costing about fifty cents, will do nicely.

The worker has by now observed this peculiarity in his bamboo-strips — that most of them are far from straight, and that their zigzag course is due mainly to *angular deflections at the knots.*   They may run fairly straight between knots, but at a knot are likely to be markedly diverted.   Our diagram is an illustration of what is meant.   In addition to

Angular deflections in stalks (and in split strips) of bamboo-cane

these angular bends, long curves are present, running in all directions.   Thus, as we sight along the strips, in some of which these irregularities are much aggravated, it would seem to be a hopeless proposition that they ever could be fashioned into a straight rod-joint.— But they can, and herein lies one of the most fascinating elements of the work.

This brings us to the consideration of another very

interesting and characteristic feature of bamboo, namely, its action under the local application of a considerable degree of *dry heat*. (It was this one point that proved the " open sesame " to satisfactory results in rod construction for the writer, and he was enabled, in return, to tell the friend who told him, about a point in gluing-up that also " straightened out " things for the friend. Until we consulted one another on these two matters each had been dissatisfied with his handiwork.) Upon holding the strip over — but not in — a gas- or oil-lamp flame, turning it the while to and fro between the fingers to expose all sides, a point is quickly reached, short of charring deeply enough to cause permanent injury, where the *fibers become so softened and pliable that all angles and sudden bends are easily straightened out* by cautious but firm manipulation between the hands; or the hot strip may be clamped straight in your vise. Immediately on cooling, the wood is *again hard, rigid, and elastic*. Professional rod-makers place the strips in a steam-box.

In this straightening, only *abrupt* deviations — whether curved or angular — need to be remedied, but *it is imperative that all such should now receive careful attention,* else later they will prevent the strips from lying *flat under pressure of the plane,* in the V-groove of the planing-mold, when cutting them down to their ultimate triangular form. All long, sweeping curves may be disregarded; these will lie flat under pressure, and largely nullify each other when six of the strips come to be bound up together. Also, it will be seen that further and very effective opportunity for straightening the whole joint presents itself when the strips are glued up.

In straightening over the flame, some considerable charring of the woody fibre on the sides of the strip *excepting its enameled surface* need not worry the novice, as all this will *plane away* in the reduction to final form — and this is why we left the rectangular strips somewhat larger than apparently was necessary; but you should take good care that this outer or rind surface is least directly exposed to the heat and so is not injured, and you do not want the rectangular strips left excessively large, else they will not bend so readily when heated as there is more wood for the heat to penetrate thoroughly.

Occasionally the sudden deflection is compound instead of simple; then it first should be reduced to a simple deflection and straightened afterward, as shown in the illustration (1, before remedying; 2, first bending; 3, direction of final bending). And here we should state that concerning the deviations

Compound lateral bend (both angular and curved deflections), viewed from rind side of strip

already noted — mostly they are angular and at the knots — we have had in mind lateral or sidewise deflections. Another condition of things may exist — generally adjacent to or between knots — vertically with relation to the enamel surface; they are sudden bumps or depressions, and the direction of the corrective bending for these then is determined according to whether they are upward or downward deflections.

Our strips now are fairly rectangular, and quite straight, at least as regards any aggravated or sudden bends. Here we again go over the knots with the file, further to modify any bumpiness at these points, when the strips are now ready for planing. It is well, first, to mark the strips at their butt ends and on the rind side, to indicate any preferable arrangement as to the order in which they shall be glued up, using the modified numerals, I, II, III, IIII, IIIII, IIIIII. These you always can decipher despite any subsequent cutting away, either at the top or bottom, in planing.

A word as to the actual significance of split *vs.* sawed strips will conclude this chapter. As already stated, the straightness of bamboo varies greatly. Some sticks may be so straight that it really would make very little difference either in the strength or action of a rod made therefrom, as to whether the rod were built from hand-rent or machine-sawed strips. But whereas in split strips the woody fibers or grain perforce must run parallel with the sides of the strip throughout its length, in the sawed strips you can have anything from astonishingly good to atrociously bad results. Of course machine sawing saves much labor, and hence is cheaper. If you have a very narrow strip that has been split out, so that you know its grain runs properly, there is no reason why you should not use a fine saw if you want to rip it lengthwise exactly through the middle, into two still slenderer strips, without risking an attempt at splitting, when you have no margin to spare. In short, from a strip that first *has been split out from the stalk,* another strip sawed out parallel to the edge of the first is every whit as good as one rent from it. In such sawing, place the strip, rind uppermost, obliquely in the vise, with the end projecting only a little above it, and saw not more than two or three inches at a time, the saw running between the jaws; then shift the strip above the vise two or three inches more, and so continue, sawing and shifting, little by little, until it is wholly divided.

The reader may judge for himself about how much of detailed care, in seasoning, selection, and utilization of material, is represented in a $2.75 department-store rod that is turned out in lots by the hundred; and yet the writer knows of one such that weathered a Nipigon campaign with flying colors. Our illustration suggests how great may be

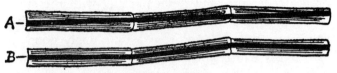

A — Sawed strip   B — Split or rent strip

the difference in the grain of two strips, one of which has been sawed by machine and the other one split or rent out of a stick by hand in the manner described and which alone guarantees the best results.

ROD-MAKING:

PLANING THE STRIPS

CHAPTER IV

ROD-MAKING:
PLANING THE STRIPS

It must be evident to anyone that in reducing roughly-squared strips of bamboo to the equilateral-triangular form and definitely-graduated taper required for their incorporation into symmetrical rod-joints, some kind of grooved form or mold is necessary for holding the strips securely and guiding the cutting exactly. Such devices have been various. They frequently are made of close-grained hard wood such as lignum-vitæ, beech, or maple. The planing-board of the professional manufacturer may be of brass.

You do not require any mold for the initial planing operations, already noted as consisting — after a mere leveling of the pith surface — simply in smoothing the split sides of each strip, where it was rent away from the parent stalk. For further *preliminary* planing and tapering, the author still makes use of the wooden mold, acceptably and quickly constructed, for this work, of any soft wood such as pine or cypress; but he never succeeded in turning out joints of satisfactory excellence until he adopted a steel mold or planing-board for the last, fine planing-down of the strips to their ultimate dimensions. Thus far the most unfavorable criticism upon this device by discerning angler friends was offered after this fashion: " Say, the joints that that thing turns out are too good; no one will believe they are hand-made, and by an amateur."

This steel mold is adjustable for the full length and varying calibers of the joints of any rod, from one having a diameter up to one inch or more at the extreme butt, if so desired, and a width at the tip of anything from a scant one-sixteenth of an inch upward. Also, the mold being made in independent halves, of not excessive rigidity, it may either be *sprung apart or compressed* along the middle — the ends first being secured — to produce a joint having either a *convex or concave taper;* or with it you may turn out simple straight-tapered joints or those hav-ing *double or combined straight tapers.* All this will be made clear as we proceed.

In employing full-length wooden molds, the usual custom is to construct a separate one for each indi-vidual joint and duplicates — butt, middle-joint, and top — of certain definite dimensions. Such a pro-cedure involves not only the extra work of making three distinct molds for each rod of a given caliber and taper, but in our experience it is far from satis-factory in that to avoid destroying the surface of the mold in the last planing, the strip surfaces — after planing them to close approximation — must be finished by filing; and it is very difficult to prevent the wearing down of the mold even in the most careful cross-filing. Such distortion of its originally even surface produces hollow places in the sides of the rod-strips, and consequently in the resultant rod-joints, and to a more aggravated degree as each succeeding strip leaves the mold. Wooden molds are further deficient in accuracy, as compared with steel molds, because the edges and angles of a wooden groove are less sharply defined than is possible with steel.

We will give sufficient details, however, of a common way of constructing wooden molds, both because we make a preliminary use of such a mold — which can thus serve us in the building of many rods of entirely different dimensions — and in order that the reader may judge how much simpler and more efficient is the process that the author personally uses and commends.

The triangles composing a hexagonal rod-section are equilateral triangles; such triangles have angles of 60 degrees, and three of them make just half of the section, comprising 180 degrees, as there are 360 degrees in a circle. It therefore is apparent that we must *plane down our strips flush with the face of a groove having an angle of 60 degrees.*

Only the *split* faces of each strip are cut down, and these by bringing them uppermost *in alternation. The rind or enamel surface lies always against one or the other side of the groove and it remains untouched by the plane.* The sketch below, of the wooden double mold, will make this clear if the text does not.

This is the way that some build the groove for the full-length mold of wood. It is made by fastening together two strips, of say ¾ inch by 1½ inches and 3½ to 4 feet long, which strips have had the proper bevel cut along the upper edges of their adjoining sides. The diagram shows how this bevel

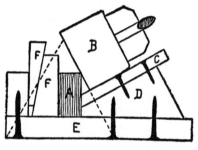

Pattern for planing-rig:

A — Mold strip
B — Plane
C — Guiding-strip
D — Brace

E — Baseboard
FF — Wedges in wedging
    space

may be cut accurately, by means of a plane, rectangular on cross-section, and which is slid along a guiding-strip that holds it tipped laterally at the proper angle. A pattern for this rig is easily made in full size by first drawing the mold-strip cross-section, A; next, getting the inclination of the bottom of the plane (B) by means of an equilateral triangle (dotted lines); then drawing at a right-angle to this the line (C) which represents the correct inclination of the guiding-strip.

The groove of such a mold is at first of a uniform depth throughout its length. To make of it a tapered groove, it remains but to plane down the face of the mold to whatever tapering depth is desired, bearing in mind that the *width of the finished groove at any point — and consequently of a surface of the bamboo-strip that will just fill the groove at the same point — is just one-half the diameter of the completed rod-joint at the corresponding point,* provided that we measure the rod's diameter from *angle to angle* of its hexagonal section, and not between opposite flat surfaces. To put it in another way, the half of a six-strip rod-joint that has been divided lengthwise presents an inside plane surface composed of only *two* adjoining surfaces, laid up edge to edge. Hence, for the sake of convenience

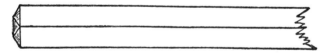

Lateral half of a hexagonal rod-joint

and clarity, we will after this speak of the *diameter from angle to angle whenever referring to rod calibers,* unless specifically designated otherwise.

This planing of the mold's grooved surface to taper is best done with a long plane that the car-

penter calls a fore-plane, and such surface should
be carefully tested lengthwise with a straight-edge
and crosswise with a try-square.

But the writer has a much simpler method than
all this, of making wooden molds for all that he requires of them. Indeed they need only approximate
accuracy; yet it is easy enough to have the angle of
the groove true. Furthermore, they *may be only
from six inches to a foot in length, the strips being
shifted along when planing them.*

The reader is now introduced to the very convenient little tool called a center-gauge. You see that
it has one pointed end and several notches, all their
angles being 60 degrees. This may be obtained

The indispensable little center-gauge

from the larger hardware stores, either untempered
or of tempered steel; you want the latter, and it will
cost about twenty-five cents. Time and again you
will find it handy for testing angles. Take your two
strips of any soft wood and plane one edge of each
approximately to the required bevel — just freehand. Place the strips side by side, the bevels facing, and test them with the point of the center-gauge.

Correct, as needed, by additional planing and testing, until the bevels and the groove they form are
fairly accurate; then, to make the groove absolutely
correct, use your tempered center-gauge as a *scraper,*
holding the tool vertically as you draw the point
lengthwise of the strips, which are paralleled but
kept slightly separated.   Now nail the beveled strips
together and your mold is ready for use.

It will be found an added convenience if you make
a double mold, by utilizing opposite surfaces of the
same strips, one groove running from about ¼-inch
deep at the large end to $\frac{3}{16}$ at the
small end, and the other being
slightly shallower.   The grain of
the wood had better run vertically,
as sketched.

Wood mold with two
grooves

Thus far the only planing of our
bamboo-strips consisted in cutting
off the pith from the inner, con-
cave side to a flat surface and the mere smoothing
of the split edges; and this preferably is done as ad-
vised, that is previous to heating and straightening
them.   The first process in actual reduction to the
triangular form wanted — and one that facilitates

Beveling one side of
strip freehand

matters when we come to make use
of the V-groove — is to lay the
strips on their sides and plane away
some more from their split faces.
As you do this, tilt the plane sideways, but only a

little, so as to make the strips narrower on the inside (pith side). We then place the strip in one or
the other of our wooden grooves — most appropriate as determined by the size of the joint under construction — with this smooth beveled edge and the
enamel surface lying against their respective sides
of the groove, and proceed to cut down the other
side to a surface *parallel with the face of the mold.*
Plane a little *first on one, then on the other* of these
split sides of the strip, alternately, until the strip
very nearly fits flush, with its enamel side up, into
this wooden groove, which is larger than the steel
groove that you will make use of for the final dress-
ing-down.

Before you reach this stage, it will however become necessary to adopt some method both of holding the strip while planing and of guarding against
cutting your fingers with the razor-like edges which
bamboo presents when cut to triangular form; for
no other holding device can compare either in simplicity or efficiency with the thumb and finger of one
hand. But if these are unprotected, as the plane
takes a firmer bite occasionally, the strip will be
pulled or pushed between the fingers and a deep and
painful cut will result, which though it may heal
readily enough, still it interferes with business. The
edges are sharp enough to make a clean cut even
though the heavy leather of an old walking-glove,
which the writer uses on his left or holding hand;

but if you wind a few turns of a one-inch gauze roller-bandage around the last joints of the thumb and forefinger of that hand before donning the glove, then you are safe and may plane away fearlessly; or a heavy canvas working-glove of the ten-cent-store species may be used.

The first planing may be done with short, rapid, overlapping strokes and with the planing-iron set rather coarse, so that it will cut comparatively short and thick shavings; but as you approach closely to the surface of your steel mold, the blade is set fine and each stroke should be *continuous* from the butt to the smaller end of the strip; there should be an even, heavy pressure on the plane, and it should be pushed ahead with slow deliberation. This last caution is all-important when planing the slender strips of delicate fly-rod top-joints, running from less than one-sixteenth inch in diameter at their butt-ends to one-thirty-secondth at their tips. There must be no backing up here, no lifting of the plane from the strip from start to finish of the stroke, as such a maneuver is likely to cause buckling and breakage of the strip. And with all planing the general rule should be regarded that applies to most cutting tools, to cut with the planing-blade *held a little obliquely*. Also see that the position of the planing-hand is not such as to obstruct the free ejection of shavings from the plane.

Early change in the position of the holding-hand,

so soon as the stroke is fully started — as illustrated in Figures 1 and 2 — is likewise an important caution to be heeded in the planing of bamboo-strips, especially for light tops. But if the accident of buckling and fracture should occur, the whole strip is not necessarily ruined for use; if cut off and pieced out with a separate section, *at exactly the point where a line-guide is subsequently to be placed,* such splinting with the guide will sufficiently reinforce it at this point so that there will be no perceptible weakness of the completed joint, as regards either action or durability.

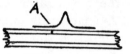

A — Point where strips join end to end, and guide serving as splint

The holding-hand, in the first position shown, must be only a few inches in advance of the plane, and it is shifted forward for subsequent strokes, as the plane closely approaches it. The strip under the plane is *pushed* against the hand so held. As the second or slenderer half of the strip is planed, the holding-hand is shifted to the second position, behind the plane; and the thumb and forefinger holding the end of the strip, which now is lifted from the groove, prevent the strip from being *pulled* ahead; and the finishing-stroke, on the smaller half, is a continuous one.

Another point in the technic here, is that of the *direction of the pressure imparted by the holding-hand's thumb and fingers.* With the plane behind

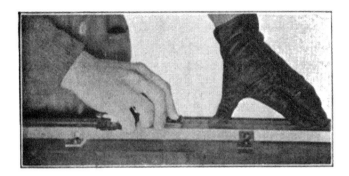

Fig. 1

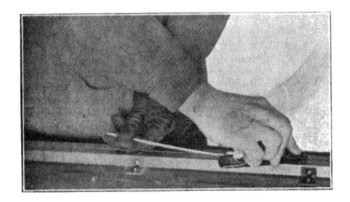

Fig. 2

Planing the Strips: Fig. 1—First position;
Fig. 2—Second position

this hand on starting to go over the strip, they should press the strip down into the groove and at the same time either to the right or left — a lateral pushing or pulling — in order to *force the rind side of the bamboo firmly against its side of the groove, and to hold it there and prevent its tilting away.* When the holding-hand is shifted to the second position, the fingers *twist* the strip toward one or the other side to accomplish the same end. Once again, heed the caution always to plane with the *plane's face parallel to the mold's surface* — not dropped either to the right or left.

If the above cautions be not observed, the result will be a strip that is irregularly triangular on cross-section, with one planed surface wider than the other, as illustrated, instead of being symmetrical, as indicated by the dotted line in the picture. To prevent a strip's thus " going off " lopsidedly, remember in your planing Lopsided strip of sides alternatingly that it is principally the *narrower* surface which requires correction in order to even up the cross-section; so make frequent observations of your work with this in mind. The endeavor should be made to have the triangular section *equilateral early in the planing and to keep it so,* rather than to permit of carelessness at first with the intention of remedying the matter later. This will save the amateur rod-builder much tribulation, as it is one of the most vital points, it being of course

impossible to make symmetrical hexagonal rod-joints
out of finished strips of irregular section.

It sometimes is convenient to correct this going
off from the true equilateral form, by again using
your center-gauge as a scraper. Fasten it upright
in the vise this time, and draw the defective strip
through its notched end, with pressure so regulated
that the scraping is done principally against the nar-
rowed side of the strip; this widens the narrow side
and at the same time narrows the side that is too
wide. V-notched truing-scrapers are easily made by
notching the edge of any piece of saw steel — as a
cabinet-makers' scraper, selling for ten cents — by
means of the common *triangular-section saw-sharp-
ening file, which has angles of the required sixty degrees.* However, if due attention is had to the
warnings already given, such corrective scraping
rarely becomes necessary.

As previously instructed, the planing-iron is set
very fine, so as to cut the thinnest possible shaving,
for the ultimate planing-down; and a few short, light
final strokes are permissible over those places felt
to be still high, as tested by drawing the finger deli-
cately across the strip and the face of the mold.
The smallest Stanley plane, about three inches long,
is very nice for this work. Keep the plane *well
sharpened* by frequent resort to the oilstone. A
few drops of thin oil placed occasionally on the metal

surface of the mold are helpful after the planing-iron begins to hug it closely.

The writer has found it sufficient for the production of accurate joints, to finish his strips entirely with the plane, except perhaps in the case of tops for the lighter fly-rods. He finishes these by scraping them lengthwise with discarded safety-razor blades, an ordinary razor-blade removed from its handle, a scissors blade, chisel, planing-iron, or a common jack-knife. Of file or sand-paper he makes no use at this stage of the work. In making his lighter top-joints, he very carefully takes off just the feather-edge at the junction of the inner sides of the strips, so that there shall be no question about their pushing home at the center of the joint when gluing up; for this delicate work the safety-razor blade is just the thing.

It now is time for the details of the metal planing- or finishing-mold itself, and the manner of its adjustment for getting out joints of the definite length and taper desired for the rod that it is determined upon to build. This is very simply constructed of two four-foot bars of ¾-inch cold-rolled steel, and it can be made at any machine-shop at moderate expense. The illustrations herewith will fully explain exactly what is wanted, and the machinist must be cautioned that the *beveled edges must be absolutely true,* in order correctly to form our sixty-

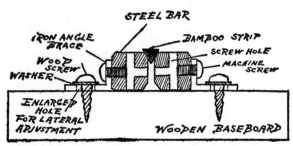

Fig. 1 — End view of author's adjustable steel planing-mold (reduced one-half)

degree-angled groove when the bars are brought together side by side.   But soon you will see that they are kept slightly apart in actual use, as our *taper is obtained by the beautifully easy stunt of spreading the separate halves of our mold obliquely and precisely to the minute fraction of an inch required.* The center-gauge will attest the mold's accuracy.

The four edges of each of our square steel bars are cut off, then, to a bevel of the same inclination, as above stated, but presenting faces of varying widths, respectively as follows: ½₂, ⅟₁₆, ⅛, and ³⁄₁₆ of an inch.   The bars are held in any degree and position of separation wanted, by means of right-angled braces, secured by appropriate screws to their respective bars, and the whole is fastened to a base of any well-seasoned wood plank about six inches in width, one inch thick, and having an unwarped surface.   The short or upright arm of the braces is ⅝ of an inch long; the long or horizontal arm is one inch; and they are one-inch wide. Machine-screws, $\frac{3}{16}$ inch in diameter and with rounding heads, secure the bar-arms of the braces to the bars. The longer arms are fastened to the wooden baseboard by one-inch wood-screws having rounded heads, and small iron washers are used under their heads. The holes in both arms of the braces are made larger than needed merely to accommodate the screws, to permit of considerable play and consequent separation of the halves of the mold. If desiring still more to increase this range of side-play of the bars, you can enlarge the screw holes in the long arms of the braces by filing them out with a small rat-tail file, thus converting these round holes into slots. Five pairs of braces, centered $10\frac{1}{2}$ inches apart, are used; and note, as shown in the Fig. 2 illustration of the mold, that it will be an added convenience in adjusting it to have the screws that secure the long arms *set to one side of those fastening the short arms*, instead of having the two sets of screws line up opposite; thus they will not interfere with each other.

The whole arrangement is at once understood by reference to the diagrammatic illustrations, Fig. 1 representing a sectional or end view, and Fig. 2 being a top view of the mold. It remains but to explain its adjustment. Suppose, for example, it is desired to make a butt-joint $3\frac{1}{2}$ feet long, having a diameter of $\frac{1}{2}$ inch at its larger end and of $\frac{3}{8}$ inch at its smaller end — measuring, please remember,

from angle to angle.   Marks on the baseboard, at
A and B in Fig. 2 will note the length of 3½ feet,
A being at the butt or larger end of the proposed
rod-joint.   (But be it understood that the *bamboo-*

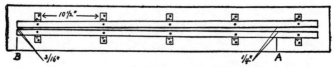

Fig. 2 — Top view of steel planing-mold

strips should be left a little longer than the com-
pleted rod-section, to allow for trimming at the
ends.)   We separate the mold-halves at this point
so that the space from bevel-edge to bevel-edge at
the mold's surface is exactly ¼ inch, or *half* the
diameter wanted there for the completed joint; and
we separate the edges ³⁄₁₆ inch at B.

The particular beveled faces or edges of the mold
that we make use of for our groove, whether one of
the narrower or wider ones, are those best facilitat-
ing the construction of a joint of the special diameter
wanted, *though the narrowest bevel may be used*
for any joint, if so desiring; we practically are un-
limited as to the larger rod-calibers that may be
produced, but the minimum is gauged by the ⅟₃₂-
inch beveled edges, which, when brought close together at one end of the mold, enable us to get out
the component strips for a top-joint ⅟₁₆ inch wide
at its tip.   But this may be further reduced when

the joint is sandpapered after gluing; and such trim-
ming-down of the small end of glued-up top-joints
may be resorted to with impunity since here we are
dealing with such a small caliber that the whole thickness of the joint is solid fiber.

Months after I had worked out the details of my
steel planing-mold and had used it with great satisfaction, it was with no little interest that I noted the
description of a " shooting-board," by G. Randle
of Plymouth, England, and communicated by him
to Mr. Marston's famous *Fishing Gazette.* As will
be seen, this is an adjustable planing-board constructed of wood. Mr. Randle says:

" During the past twelve months I have made
some half-dozen split-cane rods by means of a shooting-board made as follows: Get a piece of seasoned

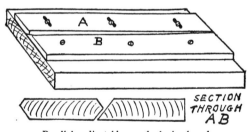

Randle's adjustable wood planing-board

yellow pine, 8 inches wide, 1½ inch thick, and 5 feet
long. Plane one side true and straight. Get two
pieces of seasoned mahogany the same length, 3
inches wide, and about 1 inch thick. Bevel the edges

as shown in the sketch. Screw these pieces to the pine board. The piece marked A is made to slide about ½ inch by cutting slots for the screws to travel in. This will allow the strips of cane to be planed of varying sections as required for the several pieces of the rod. The edges of the mahogany must be accurately beveled. Both edges of A can be beveled, one edge for the tops of the rods, the other, when reversed, for the remaining pieces."

A very practical point in rod-building that challenges attention during planing operations, is that the coarse, earlier planing is accomplished with very much greater rapidity than are the finishing-strokes, where careful deliberation must be practised; it also is very apparent how much more quickly than the smaller ones the larger joints are turned out. Again, if one job be made of the rougher planing on butt- and middle-joints for several different rods, much time is saved that otherwise would be employed in setting the planing-blade — changing from coarse to fine and back again. Then, too, it is economical to have two planes. Further, top-joints will be built by the beginner much more readily — and they will be better built — after previous experience on the larger sections. The gluing, ferrule-setting, and permanent windings likewise are much easier work for the novice when dealing with the larger joints, and previous practise here simplifies these details as applied to the more delicate tops.

From all of the foregoing the observant reader will rightly conclude that he can complete four rods, for example, if working on all four together, in much less than four times the period that would be required for one alone.   He can do all his splitting and assembling, all his rough and then the fine planing, all gluing up, the ferrule-fitting, all windings, and finally the varnishing, making a finish of each of these procedures in the order noted, and so " getting his hand in " on each that the bunch of rods is run through in a surprisingly short time.

The preliminary planing of most commercial " handmade " rods is done on a planing machine, only the final, accurate trimming of the strips being accomplished with a hand plane, when a long, jointer

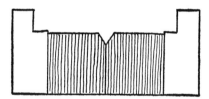

Planing-mold with side track

plane may be used.   The beveling may be done by feeding the strips to two rotary saws or cutters set at an angle of sixty degrees to each other, and the tapering accomplished by the automatic raising of a strip into the apex of the angle formed by the cutters as its small end approaches them.   In finishing up with the jointer plane, a wooden mold may be used, and the plane may travel on a track attached to the sides of the mold and which permits the planing-iron just to clear the mold's surface and thus prevents it from touching and cutting into it.

ROD-MAKING:

ROD TAPERS AND ROD PLOTTING

CHAPTER V

ROD-MAKING: ROD TAPERS AND ROD PLOTTING

The novice is now much better prepared than he was at the beginning of this discussion of rod-making, to digest profitably the somewhat more technical data regarding rod tapers, and for suggestions how to plan a rod; hence the postponement of this chapter until the present time.

A general principle that we regard as fundamental is that the butt-joint should be enough heavier than the middle-joint, and this second-joint enough heavier than the top-joint, so that the hand wielding the rod senses that it has perfect control of the rod-tip from its hold upon the handgrasp. In other words, the rod should not have the topheavy feeling imparted by a jerky top. Some foreign rods, principally of the extra long, two-handed variety for salmon fishing, are purposely thus made to give a kind of kick in throwing out the line — such as the Irish, Castleconnell rods — but personally we very much dislike this peculiarity of action.

Two split-cane rods of identical caliber and weight will rarely have exactly the same action, because the qualities of the bamboo will differ, and however little, it yet is sufficient to impart a distinctive " feel " to each one of the rods. Then, again, individual tastes differ as to just what particular feel is most acceptable; hence subtle refinements of action obtained by hollowing out the lines of a rod at one point, and by giving them a swell at another place, are worked out as the result of considerable experience both in the making and the using of rods. Therefore, beyond a certain point, it is practicable to offer data only as a basis for the reader's endeavors and not as an absolute guide.

This means that no matter how good may be the first rod put together by the beginner — and the chances are very much in favor of its being far superior to any of the cheaper ones that he can buy — that rod will not satisfy him for long; for after a thorough testing out he soon will see how he can improve upon it — or at any rate he will believe that he does. But between guiding principles and some definite detail, we can put the amateur rod-builder in possession of information sufficient to start him on his way rejoicing.

For a rod for fishing with the fly, good results may be obtained in one having a straight or even taper throughout, from butt[5] to tip; and by varying the caliber of such a rod, almost any degree of stiffness or flexibility of practical purport may be ob-

[5] " Butt " may refer to the large end of the whole rod, to the larger end of any joint or complete single section, or to the whole of the first or heaviest joint of the rod.

tained.   But a rod may be built on a swelled or convex taper, that will have a superior action; and by
looking at the diagrams below, showing just what is
meant by a straight, a compound-straight, a concave,
and a convex taper, one will immediately recognize
that the lines of the latter are the same as those
which experience has proven most acceptable for
flagstaffs and ships' spars — which also are subjected
to persistent bending strains.

Whatever the style of taper of the rest of the rod,
in any event pattern the slender top-joint after the

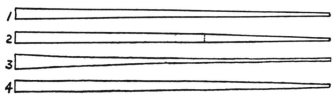

Different tapers: (1) Straight; (2) Compound straight or Scotch;
(3) Concave or hollow; (4) Convex or swelled

lines suggested by Figures 2 or 4.   It is very important for best results that the *fullness at the butt
of the top-joint be carried well forward* until about
the outer half of the joint is reached, when the caliber may fall away pretty sharply from there on to
the very tip.   As already mentioned, the extreme
outer end may be further or wholly so reduced with
sandpaper — in the case especially of the finer tops
— after gluing up.   Other methods of accomplish-
ing a similar result will be noted later on.

In planning a rod to have a straight or uniformly-graduated taper from butt to tip, the caliber of that rod at any cross-section throughout its length is readily determined by means of a diagram plotted as we will now explain; and even if it be not intended to have your rod of an absolutely uniform taper, such a diagram nevertheless furnishes a convenient basis for whatever modifications may be determined upon, and lets the reader into the secret of how he may design a rod of any taper or combination of tapers desired.

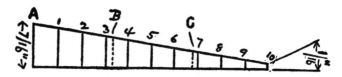

Taper diagram for plotting rod

Say that we have in mind a fly-rod of ten feet in length, of $\frac{7}{16}$ inch diameter where the butt joins the handgrasp, and $\frac{1}{16}$ inch at the tip.   We will reduce it to a drawing in this way, each quarter-inch of *length* in our illustration representing one foot of actual rod-length.   In practise we prefer to have the drawing on a larger scale, so that each $1\frac{1}{2}$ inches represents a foot, when $\frac{1}{8}$ inch then represents an inch of the real rod and $\frac{1}{16}$ inch stands for a half-inch.   The *diameters* of your rod are the *actual lengths* of these cross-lines of your diagram, at the

cross-sections marked respectively 1, 2, 3, 4 feet,
etc., from the butt end.

Next we must get the diameters of the respective
ends of our middle-joint, the rod being composed of
three joints or pieces; and for the reason that we
prefer all three *completed* joints to be of the same
length, and because allowance must be made for the
ferrule lengths, this is not so absolutely simple as it
might seem. For perfect accuracy in our figures
certain ferrule lengths must be known before we can
ascertain the diameters of the joints at the points
where the selected ferrules are to be located.

The butt male (inner or center) ferrule of the
middle-joint will be seated about 1¼ inches in the
female or outer ferrule at the smaller end of the
butt-joint, and the top-joint ferrule will seat about
1⅛ inches in its companion half; thus the total length
of the rod when jointed up will be 2⅜ inches shorter
than the total length of its three joints or parts if
placed simply end to end, without engaging the ferrules. We want a total length, *jointed,* of ten feet
or 120 inches; then we must have a total length, un-
jointed, of 122.375 inches, to be divided equally into
three parts. This gives 40.79 inches for each completed joint, *including the projecting ferrules.* The
female or projecting ferrule of the first- or butt-joint
reaching 1¼ inches (the depth that the male half
seats) beyond the wood, gives 40.79 less 1¼, or
39.54 inches, for the actual wood length of that

joint (it being understood that some ten to twelve inches of handgrasp are included in this joint, in the completed rod); the corresponding ferrule-half of the second-joint projecting 1⅛ inches, leaves that amount less than 40.79, or 39.665 inches, for the wood length of the second-joint. The way that it works out is shown in our next illustration.

Going back now to our previous diagram, we measure 39.54 inches from A, which gives B as

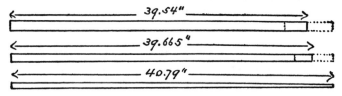

Finding the joint wood-lengths — 10-foot rod

the actual common caliber of the adjoining ends of the first- and second-joints; measuring, once more, 39.665 inches from the point B, gives us C as the remaining caliber wanted.   We now know the *length of each of our bamboo-joints irrespective of the ferrules,* and we know the *diameters of the respective ends of these joints or pieces of the rod,* and can proceed to set our metal grooved-mold accordingly, using *half of each of these diameters as the measurements from bevel-edge to bevel-edge across the face of the mold,* in getting out the component joint-strips.   Of course we maintain the mold so set, by tightening up the screws.

The reader might be interested to learn what analysis of the lines of some of the best professional-made rods would reveal as to tapers. We are pleased that we can satisfy this very natural curiosity. The rods that the author calipered, at every foot throughout their lengths, are respectively the most famous American and British makes. The former is eight feet long and weighs three and one-half ounces; the latter is nine and one-half feet and weighs six and one-quarter ounces (a dry-fly rod). Each five-eighths of an inch in length of the diagram represents one foot of rod-length. The actual diameters that the rods calipered at each foot of their individual lengths are indicated by the figures in fractions of an inch. By multiplying these by four (in the original drawing), we obtained — in an exaggerated form, for easier perception — the widths which, connected by the solid longitudinal lines, give the lines of the rods; and these may be compared with the dotted lines in the diagram, which represent straight-tapered rods.

Another clue to some of the underlying principles of successful rod-construction is furnished by noting the *point of balance* — where the rod will balance when held at one point horizontally, as across the finger — in some of the highest-grade productions. In two famous makes of American rods, tested without attached reel, Mr. Charles Zibeon Southard gives these figures: 31 inches from the butt end of

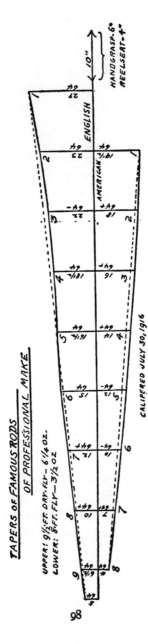

TAPERS OF *FAMOUS RODS*
OF *PROFESSIONAL MAKE*

UPPER: 9½ FT. DRY FLY — 6¼ OZ.
LOWER: 8 FT. FLY — 3½ OZ

CALIPERED JULY 30, 1916

HANDGRASP - 6"
REELSEAT - 4"
10"

ENGLISH

AMERICAN

98

handgrasp, in a 9-foot rod weighing 3½ ounces; 31½ inches, in a 9½-foot rod weighing 4 ounces; 34⅞ inches, in a 10-foot rod weighing 5 ounces. Rods from the other maker showed: 31¼ inches, in a 9½-foot rod weighing 4½ ounces; and 34½ inches, in a 10-foot rod weighing 5¾ ounces. The increased weight of the handgrasp in a detachable-handle rod — because of the extra ferrule — would bring the balancing-point or center of gravity nearer to the butt end.

In the endeavor to copy in a duplicate the exact action of any particular rod, these balancing-points should coincide; so, too, should the extent of the vertical deflection from the horizontal of the respective tips, under the influence of a definite weight attached — say of one or two ounces — when the butts of the jointed-up rods are held securely; and further, so should the rate of the vibrations of the rods be the same when, still held as above, they are set to working. Says Mr. Ralph L. Montagu of Oroville, Calif.: " In order to make this test, the handle of the fully-jointed rod should be held in a vise " or blocked up on the end of a table and " firmly held by an assistant. Now, by pressing down on the rod near the handle, get it vibrating up and down; as soon as the vibrations become regular, get out your watch and count the number per minute, using a finger to touch the rod lightly each time it comes up, and thus continuing its full swing."

The downward deflection of the tip from the horizontal without any weight attached is termed the " free deflection."   Mr. Montagu gives the following data concerning " a very perfect dry-fly rod made by a manufacturer with a world-wide reputation: Length, 9½ feet; weight, 6 ounces; free deflection, 6 inches; deflection with 1-ounce weight, 19½ inches, with 2-ounce weight, 33 inches; vibrations per minute, 106."   The stiffer the rod the " quicker " it is — the more vibrations per minute; the " soft " rod is a " slow " one.   " A good rod should have not less than one-hundred vibrations per minute."   We also might note here that for best results in a rod designed for dry-fly fishing it is enlarged or made extra stocky toward the extreme butt.

When it comes to a rod for bait-fishing, and to the construction of a short, Western-style rod for casting artificial bait from the reel, better results are attained for the special work required if these rods are relatively stiffer at the tip and for some distance back than obtains in a fly-rod.   We will achieve this effect by having a more markedly divergent taper near the lighter end.   In the case of our ten-foot fly-rod, as plotted — which is a rod having considerable backbone — a very satisfactory result will be produced by making an additional, bait top that shall be just one foot shorter than the fly top-joint, and by tapering it in a swelled fashion from the caliber at

C to from 2½ to 3/32 of an inch in diameter at its tip.

You will want two fly tops and two bait tops for this rod, top-joints being always supplied in duplicate with rods from the dealer's as they are the parts most frequently broken. Sample dimensions for the short, bait-casting rod mentioned above will be given later.

We now have planned a ten-foot fly-rod weighing about seven ounces and suitable for heavy fresh-water angling, which with its shorter and stiffer top makes a very effective nine-foot bait-rod. For a second, lighter but very serviceable all-around fly-rod, the writer advises one of nine feet, having a butt caliber of 3/8 inch at the handgrasp junction and measuring 1/16 inch at tip; and a more flexible rod, of very sweet action but still having plenty of " ginger ", is achieved by using the same size ferrules while drawing the rod out to a total length of nine and one-half feet, the extra six inches representing an addition at the butt — which somewhat increases the diameter just above the grasp — and especial care being taken to see that the full diameters of the whole of the butt-joint are not skimped.

To secure the nicest action for fly-rods, do not have the diameter at the butt end of the butt-joint any oversize (unless deliberately so for special, dry-fly work) ; the same caution applies with even more emphasis to the top end of the middle-joint; but be sure to have the butt end of the top-joint fully up to the measure, and to lighten the outer half of this section as already mentioned. The reason why the delicate top-joint of a properly-proportioned rod that is skilfully handled is sufficient to withstand all legitimate stress, is because a steadily-increasing strain is continuously thrown back upon the stronger parts of the rod. But when the butt of the top-joint is too slender and joins with a middle-joint small end that is too stiff, then the strain on the top is not progressively and properly transferred to the middle-joint, which is the prime factor in the rod's action. A weak middle-joint means a vitally weak rod, irrespective of any other features, and it means a rod with a " kick." Also be it understood that owing to the *bracing and distributing, truss effect of the line strung through the guides* of a rod, the rod will bear much more strain than if the line simply were fastened to its tip.

The reader will be interested to know what is meant by a " double-built " rod. This construction includes twelve instead of six strips to a joint, for a hexagonal cross-section, and the diagram illustrates their arrangement. It might at first glance seem that this involves just double the work in planing and gluing, but such is not the case. To produce this joint, the builder proceeds simply to glue together two thinner bamboo-strips to make the rectangular strip, preliminary to planing to the triangular shape. After filing the knots, and straightening his strips, he planes down a half-dozen on the pith side to but half the full thickness wanted. The other six strips, after receiving the same treatment, he *files crosswise on the* *enamel side* just enough to flatten this surface for a glue joint; the plane will not bite efficiently on this glossy, outside surface of the bamboo. When glued together, each double or compound strip will present on cross-section the appearance shown. The

Cross-section of double-built joint

 further treatment of these double strips is identical with that of simple strips, as already detailed, the result being as the dotted V of the illustration. In gluing together the halves of each strip, the knots are slipped or staggered as well as when gluing up the completed strips into joints.

A double or compound strip

There is one situation where the expedient of double-built joints is of practical advantage, and that is in building butt- and middle-joints of very large caliber — as for salmon or salt-water rods. It also will be the resort at any time when you desire to construct a solid-fiber butt-joint and when a single thickness of the stock on hand is scant for the purpose. You also can employ this method in combining the handsomer Calcutta bamboo on the outside, for looks, with the Tonkin on the inside of the joints, for service, making the Calcutta strips exceedingly thin — a mere veneer. Double-built construction is not practicable for top-joints except the very heaviest.

A brief description here of the various classes of rods, their dimensions and distinctive uses, will be appropriate. Rods for fresh-water angling comprise trout fly-rods, salmon rods, bait-rods, and the Kalamazoo or short rod that in recent years has been designated as the " bait-casting " rod. Certain kinds either of live or artificial bait are properly cast with the standard, long bait-rod — and at times the quarry is thus more pleasurably played, and in a manner more sportsmanlike; but the distinctive appellation of " bait-casting " rod has come to denote a stiffish, short implement, preferably between the length limits of five to six feet, and which is used for casting particularly the heavier kinds of artificial bait — more frequently a wooden minnow or some other form of " plug " — the line running directly from a quadruple-multiplying reel as the cast is made. It is a Western style, very effective in bass fishing under certain conditions, is favored by many anglers for maskinonge in preference to trolling, and has been adopted to some extent even for trout and for salt-water fishing. It requires a distinctive and very interesting technic, and the sport also is similar to fishing with the artificial fly in that the angler goes after his fish instead of waiting for the fish to come to him.

The salmon rod is an overgrown trout fly-rod, suited for its use in killing the larger and heavier fish. Salmon fishing has been much more extensively indulged in abroad than in the United States; consequently the prevailing popular style of salmon tackle was until somewhat recently dictated wholly by the ideas of foreign makers, principally English, Scotch, or Irish. These formerly were accustomed to produce absurdly formidable affairs in salmon rods, running to twenty feet in length and weighing several pounds. But the influence of the combined elegance and efficiency of the lighter, American trout-rods was reflected in the sphere of salmon-fishing tackle, so that now one rarely finds a rod of over sixteen feet in the hands of a modern salmon-angler; and many of them are shorter than this. Thus a recent number of the London *Fishing Gazette* tells about one British angler writing another: " I once owned an 18-foot greenheart salmon-rod, but induced a naval officer, ordered to British Columbia, to accept it as a present — sheer luck this, of course. I also owned two 17-footers; one of these a friendly Hussar put permanently out of business the first morning he borrowed it, but the other one I can neither sell nor lose, and keep for lending to friends, with the result that they soon buy rods for themselves. This would really suit you admirably if you 'd care to buy it cheap; it 's by a leading Scotch maker, and being twenty years old is thoroughly seasoned. I have three 16-footers. One was originally bought for mahseer and is too powerful for most any other fish. Another was given to me by J. F. G., nearly twenty years ago, when he took entirely to split-cane. It was washiba wood — since furnished with greenheart butt and top — made by Harold, of Mallow. It has killed its thousandth fish and is my favorite rod. The third is also a daisy, by Farlow, in two splices. But I am getting on towards middle-age, and want a ' de luxe ' rod. These 16-footers of mine weigh 42 ounces, 39 ounces, and 38¾ ounces, respectively. Now Hardy's split-bamboo 16-footers weigh from 28 to 32 ounces. True, their price is a stomachache, but — well — perhaps to celebrate peace —."

The best British casting records made with rods of any length have been exceeded by American casters with fifteen-foot rods, weighing about twenty-five ounces. Both hands are used on the rod in making the cast with the typical salmon-rod; it is a two-handed rod, and the butt and grasp are modified accordingly.

We will now note some of the standard sizes and weights of different kinds of modern fresh-water bamboo rods, omitting extended reference to trolling-rods because the bait-casting rod with longer and heavier top answers every purpose for this style of angling. The figures given are subject to some slight changes owing to the varying weights of different samples of bamboo-cane, and to differences in the windings and metal fittings of completed rods. The style of handgrasp and whether a rod is fitted with metal (solid) reelseat or simple reel-bands (skeleton reelseat) also are important modifying factors of the total weight. According to the rules of tournament casting, three-quarters of an ounce may be deducted from the total weight either for a solid reelseat or for the extra pair of ferrules necessitated with the independent grasp. Keeping these qualifications in mind, we may make the general statement that fly-rods for trout and bass fishing range from eight feet in length and weighing four ounces, to eleven feet with a weight of nine ounces; though a ten-foot rod weighing seven ounces, or not much more, will, except in rare instances, be the advisable extreme for heavy rods of this class. For bass fishing, we recommend nothing under nine feet, and weighing six ounces — or five and one-half at the very least. An 8½-foot rod ordinarily weighs about 4½ ounces; one of 9½ feet, 6 ounces; and of 10½ feet, 8 ounces. Rods *are* made to weigh much under these figures; split-bamboos have been constructed, from seven to eight feet in length, that would scale *one and three-quarters ounces* — perchance even less, for all we know. It hardly is necessary to state that such phenomenally light creations are suitable only for the maker's exhibit of his technical skill or as pretty toys for the collection of the financially plethoric anglermaniac.

As to calibers, the 8- and $8\frac{1}{2}$-foot rods will measure about $\frac{9}{32}$ of an inch at the extreme butt end and a scant $\frac{2}{32}$ at the extreme tip; the same sizes of ferrules, $\frac{17}{64}$ inch and $\frac{5}{32}$, will be used for both. Nine- and $9\frac{1}{2}$-foot rods will be $\frac{11}{32}$ to $\frac{13}{32}$ inch at butt and $\frac{2}{32}$ to $2\frac{1}{32}$ at tip; and will take ferrules of $\frac{17}{64}$ or $\frac{18}{64}$ and $\frac{11}{64}$ inch. Ten- to 11-foot rods will measure from $\frac{13}{32}$ to $\frac{15}{32}$ inch at butt and from $2\frac{1}{32}$ to $\frac{3}{32}$ inch at tip; taking ferrules of either $\frac{19}{64}$, $\frac{21}{64}$ or $\frac{22}{64}$ and $\frac{12}{64}$, $\frac{13}{64}$ or $\frac{14}{64}$ inch. *The actual diameters of stock ferrules may vary minutely from their sizes as listed by the dealer.*

With rods from twelve to sixteen feet in length, we are in the salmon class. Such rods, if built double, will be proportionately heavier than according with the above schedule, because of the greater weight of the enamel or denser fiber.

For calipering rods and for determining the diameters of the ferrules required in individual cases, some form of accurate calipering instrument is quite indispensable. The handiest form for the rod-worker is that like a miniature monkey-wrench, gauged to measure 64ths of an inch, and it costs about two dollars at the hardware store.

The short, bait-casting rod is sometimes made in one piece or joint; either with or without an inde-

Rod calipers

pendent handgrasp. The writer prefers here the
short butt-joint with solid handgrasp and long top
arrangement; and he makes two top-joints, one being lighter than the other for the casting of the
lighter lures, and each is in duplicate.

As to details of construction relating to the specific styles and arrangements of guides for all of
these rods, these will be considered in the chapter on
" Windings and Guides."

The bait-casting rod is 5¼ feet in length, divided
as follows: handgrasp and reelseat, 10 inches; top-
joint, 38¼ inches. The butt-joint is a scant 7⁄16 inch in

Bait-casting rod layout

diameter at its larger end (A) and $^{21}/_{64}$ inch at the
other (B); and the top-joints are each $^{7}/_{64}$ inch at
their tips, but differently tapered, though each has a
double or divergent taper.

We spoke awhile ago of giving a double taper to light fly-rod top-joints by sandpapering down the outer part after the joint was glued.   Another way to achieve practically the same thing is by a swelled taper obtained by *springing the mold apart a bit when setting it for getting out the individual strips of the joint;* this is conveniently done by twisting a screwdriver the blade of which is thrust between its halves.   Or, again, you can make double-tapered tops in the way that we have done it particularly with the heavier, bait-casting rod top-joints.   The

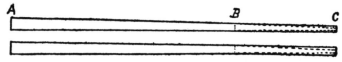

Double or compound straight-tapered top-joints

diagram will make this third method clear.   These two tops first are planed down on a simple straight taper — that is, their component strips are — in either case the mold being set at 10½/64 inch for the butt end.   In building the lighter top, we first set the mold for ⅚₄ inch at the tip (C in the upper drawing), 38¼ inches from A.   For the heavier top, the mold first is set at ⅚₄ inch at C.   The point B is at the location of a pair of the braces which hold the halves of the mold securely at the degree of separation at which they are adjusted, and it is about thirteen inches from C.   In completing the planing of the strips for either top, we then loosen up all the baseboard brace-screws *excepting the two which hold the mold at* B; we then *pinch together the ends of the mold,* at C, this time setting it here for 3½/64 inch, and then plane the second, outer taper, from B to C. In getting the exact desired width for setting the small end of the mold, it sometimes is convenient — when double-tapering joints in this way — to use a certain number of pieces of tin or cardboard of a definite thickness and to bring the halves of the mold tight up against these " shives " when placed between their ends.

No special attention other than the present reference will be paid to rods especially designed for lt-water angling, as such implements are more frequently made of material other than bamboo because of the corrosive effect of sea water on fine tackle. Furthermore, sufficient additional data as to patterns and dimensions are easily obtained from the catalog of any first-class tackle-house; and yet again, are these really worthy of being considered " rods? " Rather, should they not be regarded in the light of mere infant telegraph-poles? (— Who threw that tarpon!) Be that as it may, nobody who has mastered the principles of constructing angling-rods of split-bamboo has anything to worry about in such a straight-away proposition as the making of solid-wood rods, of greenheart, bethabara, lance-wood, hickory, ash, or in some combination of these. Such materials, in the square, and of sizes suitable for the various joints, are stocked by tackle-men, as also are spring-butts and other two-handed grasps. However, in concluding this chapter, we will note a simple device that we have found useful in reducing square rod-wood to tapered joints in the square. You then can place the joints in a wooden grooved-holder and plane off the edges to convert the tapered square joint into a tapered octagonal joint. The remaining work, of making a rounded swelled-taper joint or whatever kind is wanted, is all done with steel crescentic-notched scrapers (you can make them with a rat-tail file) and sandpaper, manipulated lengthwise of the joints as they at the same time are kept revolving by the other hand.

The top view of this tapering device is shown in Fig. 1. The sides are of wood, three inches

Fig. 1 — Top view of tapering-rig for solid-wood rods

wide and one-half inch thick, held about the same distance apart — or slightly more — by the blocks set between the ends. Another piece of board, which fits snugly the space between the other two but is short enough to permit tilting of its ends, simply is slipped in. It is an easy matter to adjust this loose board, and to hold it by ordinary clamps which squeeze it at either end between the outer boards, in such position that you can reduce a squared stick that is laid against its upper edge, and held between the outside boards, to any taper desired, by planing the stick down flush with the upper edges of these outside boards (see Fig. 2).   While doing

Fig. 2 — Side view of tapering-rig

this, the whole affair is held in your bench-vise. The side boards of this rig — or at least their upper edges — are preferably made of fine-grained hard wood; all else may be of any soft wood.

ROD-MAKING:

GLUING UP

CHAPTER VI

ROD-MAKING: GLUING UP

The attempt at gluing up his rod-joints has proven the particular Slough of Despond in which the creative ambition of many a prospective rod-builder has become hopelessly mired; so it is not without a full sense of the responsibility assumed that we begin this chapter. Yet despite all this — listen, brother, while we whisper it — the writer of these words has glued, does and can glue up rod-joints — glue them up *straight,* and without suffering paralyzing apprehension as to the outcome while engaged in the process. Therefore take heart, all ye fearful ones.

Various recommended methods were given trial before formulating the technic which has worked out most successfully in our own case, and which we shall conscientiously explain.

What are the customary directions and suggestions — and their inevitable complications? — about as follows: First, you are told that both glue and strips must be kept hot; then, that it is necessary that the strips should receive a preliminary bath of glue which is allowed to dry in the bamboo, filling its pores; that you must heat a little and wind a lit-

tle; that the winding — this temporary winding coincident with gluing — especially in the case of the
lighter joints and tops, will give a spiral twist to the
joint — which you must overcome by winding in the
opposite direction, and crossing the first threads,
back to the starting-point; and if, before you get a
quarter of the distance on your return trip, the glue
has cooled and set so that the twist does *not* come
out as you were counting on, why you heat the joint
again (perhaps over an oil- or gas-stove or with a
" steam hose "), and repeat as often as may be necessary — your fingers the while accumulating stratified
layers of rapidly congealing glue, so that they stick to
each other and to the bamboo more tightly than the
strips seem inclined to stick together — and there is
glue, glue everywhere, particularly where you least
want it, and where it most effectually can obstruct the
work in hand.   Yes, it *is* fierce!

You may be interested to learn that Divine, the
Utica, N. Y., rod-maker, once cataloged a special
rod having a permanent torsional twist put deliberately into it, and he claimed that joints so made are
more rigid than those of the standard form of construction.   Accept whatever of consolation this bit
of information may bring.   We note also that the
addition of a little acetic acid or vinegar to the glue
has been recommended for retarding its gelatiniza-
tion or setting; personally, we have not found the
expedient necessary.

In applying the glue to the strips, perhaps you have stood them endwise in a tin-tube of glue — standing that in hot water to keep it warm — and winding first one end of the joint and then reversing it and winding the other; or, first having tied the strips together at two or three points, you have made use of a cardboard or tin device having a circle of six triangular holes through which the unglued strip-ends are thrust to keep them separated while applying the glue to their individual inner surfaces, as you intermittently glue for a short distance, slip the separator along a bit, and wind. Then, after the winding is completed, from butt to the smaller end of the joint, you sight along the joint for irregularities, and heat it again at these points, to correct them by counter-bending.

Again, we have tried gluing up and winding the joints in separate halves, clamping each half till the glue had thoroughly set, and then gluing the mating halves together and clamping the whole against a rigid, straight, heavy strip of wood with a lighter clamping strip. This latter plan yielded pretty fair results with some larger joints.

But whatever of routine success others may have achieved in pursuance of any of the above methods, certain it is for us that way lies despair and wrathful objurgation, nothwithstanding we are able to endure all the preceding stress of splitting, straightening, and planing with unruffled placidity.

Most assuredly, if it be possible to glue and wind joints so that most of the glue remains where it is wanted, and with but a minimum thereof affectionately attaching to the hands, and if the joints can be wound in one direction only, and all this be accomplished while at the same time *straightening instead of twisting* the joints, such a technic is highly desirable from all standpoints — those of progress, comfort, and efficiency. We presently will explain our path to this end. It is not to be expected, however, from any method of gluing, that the meekest gluer may avoid becoming palpably " stuck-up." But a little hot water readily removes the glue from your hands — if not its remoter effects from your conscience — which thus should be unburdened at sundry interludes, as shall faithfully be noted.

We are reminded here of the illuminating reply received by one who was attempting to lure from a professional rod-maker, canny as famous, the exact details of his gluing process. The query, " By the way, Tom, how do you glue up? " elicited: " Why, how do you suppose? With *glue,* of course." The anecdote serves as an introduction to the subject of glue itself.

The descriptive catalogs of most rod-manufacturers will tell how each one's brand of rod is made with a special, secret " waterproof cement," of wonderful adhesive and cohesive qualities; how even the bamboo employed is of a particularly superior variety which needs must receive a distinguishing appellation unknown to the botanists; and how the varnish used is unlike anything in the varnish line known in the regular trade. In short — and similarly with particular brands of automobiles, marine gas-engines, guns and a few other articles of merchandise — this particular rod, sold by this particular house, is the one and only implement, embodying to a superlative degree all the attainable excellencies to which an angling-rod could lay claim.

Now, all these are good rods; and there can be no question that there are various and valuable trade secrets peculiar to rod-making, just as there are in any matured manufacturing industry — yet, glue is glue; and it is perfectly well understood by sophisticated buyers that in a general way such assertions of unique excellence may be dismissed as mere trade " talking-points."

Any ordinarily good glue will suffice. The writer even has glued up satisfactory joints with the sheet gelatine that you buy in grocery stores for kitchen use, dissolved in hot water. Appropriately enough, genuine Russian isinglass — fish glue — is stated to be the very best thing for the purpose. It ought to be, at the price quoted, which years ago was about seven dollars a pound. It is made from the bladder of the sturgeon, the real article is very difficult to obtain, and many cheaper forms of gelatine are so called. The reader is at liberty to seek this elusive

brand,[6] or to obtain the more expensive grade of
imported French or German glue, soaking it over-
night in cold water to soften it, then boiling it up in
a regulation glue-pot when ready to apply it, and
thus preparing it afresh each time that it is used —
if he wants to.

Many practical carpenters use Le Page's prepared liquid glue in their work, and we have glued
rod-joints with this also. With Major's cement,
Jeffrey's marine glue, and liquid " iron cement " we
have had no experience in this connection. From
any pattern- or cabinet-maker you can obtain some
glue — perhaps coarsely granular and often comprising broken pieces of many different samples — that
will serve your purpose fully. And after a short preliminary soaking in cold water, you can add a little
more, hot water and boil it up by placing its cheap
tin-container in a second receptacle, an ordinary
saucepan of water. Some rod-makers' choice is a
good quality of white glue. In any event it should
boil slowly — simmer — and the longer it cooks the
better will it be; and a hide glue is superior to a bone
glue. Any expert wood-worker will tell you that
two other important factors of an A-1 gluing job are
that the *glue should be used thin and that the wood is
hot* when glued. Professionals heat the bamboo-
strips in a hot-box.

The amateur rod-builder can get a good fire go-

6 Try Eimer and Amend's, New York. Some of this glue may be mixed
with other glue.

ing in the kitchen range, place two irons or bricks a foot or so apart, and with thin pieces of wood topping them, on the stove over the fire (stove cover-holes remaining closed), and lay his strips athwart these wood supports till hot, without injury. Or a kitchen gas-range may be used, by placing the irons or bricks with a sheet of tin over them to cover two holes, and laying the pieces of wood to hold the strips atop the tin.

While the function fulfilled by the glue in binding the strips together is tremendously effective from the standpoint of the increased rigidity of the glued joint as compared with its strips when simply bound together by windings, it nevertheless is true that all the glue has to accomplish is to hold the strips from sliding one against another — that is, to prevent them from acting individually instead of as a solid homogeneous piece, when a bending strain is applied. Now, a very slight adhesive force between the strips will suffice for this when it is distributed along their whole length, especially when this bond is supplemented by the ferrules at the ends of the joints, by the line-guide wrappings, and by the other strong, permanent silk-windings held in a plentiful coating of varnish.

The malleability of the joints, and just how they act before the glue has stiffened, may be well observed in a joint whose finished strips are assembled and held by a snug temporary winding, without any glue having been applied as yet. Both the winding and the yet soft glue permit the strips to slide, one upon another, as you bend the joint; and to remain approximately in whatever was the form when the bending force was interrupted, because also they hold the strips from slipping back into their original position, until a counteracting force is applied. Bend the joint into an S shape and so it remains until bent some other way. Thus it is that *this time of gluing up is the most advantageous time for molding the completed joints straight.*

Get a small camel's-hair brush, not over one-half inch wide — or better, the stiffer, Siberian ox-hair kind that paint stores carry — and have your glue in readiness, the container resting in the saucepan of water which is kept warm over a convenient oil- or gas-heater or on the kitchen coal-range. Loose

Doubled winding-thread with noose

the strips of your joint from the winding that has bound them since they were finished. The writer uses Barbour's linen-thread — obtained at the dry-goods store — number 25 for all except top-joints, and number 40 for these; and he makes use of the one piece for temporary binding and for the winding-thread used in gluing. This thread, doubled, and made long enough to wind the whole length of the joint, has a slip-noose turned in its looped end.

Place the thread conveniently nearby, so you can
grab it instantly when wanted. Also have handy
some warm water in a basin, a sponge, and a piece
of rag (no relation to the " bone and hank of
hair ").

Lay the strips down in front of you, arranged in
two groups of three strips each, and in this order:

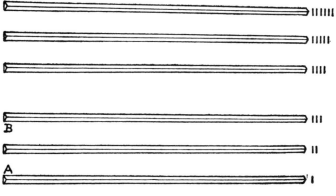

Strips grouped ready for gluing

Pick up strip number I in your left hand, grasping
it near its middle, and rapidly but thoroughly, with
long strokes, apply the warm glue to the whole
length of the inside surface, A, beginning at the
smaller end; then lay the strip down again, on its
remaining dry, planed surface. (It is better that
the room where these sacred rites are progressing
should be decidedly warm — at night, when the rest
of the family are all abed, in the kitchen on the

table, which is drawn near to the coal-range, after you have started that a-going at a good pace, is ideal.) Next, treat strip number III (no, we don't mean II) in the same way, applying the glue to its planed surface B; lay it down. At any time when the brush may stiffen or the glue in the brush is too thick to spread well, limber the brush and thin the glue a bit at one and the same time by cleaning out the brush in the hot water in which the glue-can sits. Now you may pick up strip II and cover *both* of its planed surfaces with glue; and *don't* lay this down — yet — but transfer it to your right hand (having laid that brush in a *safe place,* mind you, from where it will not fall on the floor and annex a choice collection of dust), which grasps it between thumb and forefinger, at the butt. Next, seizing strip I similarly in the left hand, pick it up and bring the glued sides of the strips II and I together; and, then, holding both in the left hand, pick up strip III and bring that up against the first two. Then place this half-section on the table, with planed surfaces down, and pinch all three strips together firmly, along their whole length, between thumbs and fingers, sufficiently for them to adhere together as a unit — some gaping will do no harm.

Now, wash your hands in the warm water in the basin and wipe them on the rag.

Exactly the same maneuvers are repeated with

strips IIII, IIIIII, and IIIII, and this second half-joint is placed on the table near the first.

Repeat the hand washing.

Return to the half-section first glued, turn it on its back and spread glue liberally over its whole uppermost or inside surface, which is two strips wide. Apply glue similarly to the second half; and bring these halves together.

Be *sure* to wash your hands this time, before proceeding with the next steps, which are as follows: First secure the joint halves tightly at the butt with the noosed end of your doubled thread; but before pulling the noose up snug, tap the butt of the joint smartly against the table to even up the ends of all the strips. (Here's where you begin to speed up a bit — and where in Sam Hill *is* that blooming thread? — Well, we told you to have it handy, didn't we?) Having gripped the whole joint firmly within the noose, take a few initial spiral turns *away from you,* around the joint (Fig. 1). Next, turn the joint so that its butt is now directed toward your left hand; *lay it down on the table,* still holding taut on the winding-thread; and proceed to wind tightly in spirals, spaced about three-eighths of an inch; *rolling the joint away from you as you simultaneously pull the thread toward you, and force all the strip edges evenly together* under the combined constriction of the progressively encircling winding,

the rolling of the joint, and the downward pressure
against the table of the palmar surface of the fingers
of both hands (Fig. 2).

Before proceeding very far you will note to your
great surprise and delight, first, that as you wind,
the joint is *straightened by being rolled against the
unyielding level surface of the table;* and, next, that
it *does not twist* when carefully wound in this way,
but each of its six flat surfaces holds to its own
proper plane.

Having completed the winding, wipe off the excess of glue with the sponge and a little hot water.
This also wets and shrinks the winding-thread, making still tighter constriction.   Sight now along the
joint for the more noticeable deflections; correct
these by counter-bending, take out any very mild
twist by counter-twisting, and then submit the whole
joint to some more *rolling treatment, very vigorously
now,* to and fro under the palms of the hands (Fig.
3), and bearing on with considerable pressure.   Occasionally we have rolled a joint under a flatiron.
Continue rolling until the glue is well set and the
joint considerably stiffened up, which requires only
a few minutes, when it may be allowed to repose on
the table until morning.

Yes, it's pretty late — but really you should wash
your hands again before going to bed.

The following day you may remove the winding-
thread and sandpaper the joint, using number o or

Gluing Up: Fig. 1—Starting the winding-thread

Gluing Up: Fig. 2—Winding

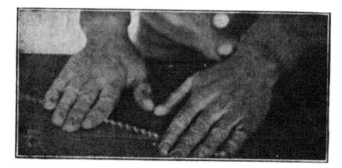

Gluing Up: Fig. 3—Rolling

number 1 paper. First remove the hardened ex-
uded glue by systematically going lengthwise over
each of the six flat surfaces individually; then over
the joint as a whole, just sufficiently for the removal
of any remaining glue and for the slightest rounding of its edges; except that the outer part of fly-
rod top-joints may be sandpapered vigorously to materially reduce the caliber here as noted in the previous chapter.

Sight along the cleaned joint once more; correct
any slight deflections yet remaining, by heating them
very carefully over the flame (the enamel surface is
bound to be exposed toward the flame now), manipu-
lating them between the fingers, and once more doing a little rolling, with the pressure concentrated
at the particular spot undergoing final treatment.

And there you are! Rod-building possesses no
more difficulties for you, worthy of the name; your
joint is glued up; it has become a thing of beauty,
as straight as an arrow. Who now may say that
you can't do the trick?

At this stage we once again take note of any little
lumpiness that may still remain at the knot-sites, and,
where indicated, make a final application of the file,
using this time the small triangular saw-file and not
the coarse, cross-hatched tool.

Having glued up our joints they now are ready
to be fitted with their respective ferrules. They are
straight and rigid, and should remain lying on a flat

surface or suspended from their ends while awaiting
further attention; do not allow them to stand on
end, the ends only being supported, or they may become bowed.   And as varnish is an effective preventive against the absorption of dampness, and the
subsequent warping due to this cause, we apply the
first coat very soon, but invariably on a *dry day*.   It
also is our personal practise to invest the joints with
their first permanent, silk windings — after the manner described under " Windings and Guides "— before they receive this first varnishing.

A professional method of gluing and winding
known to the author as having been employed by
at least one maker, is the following: The six strips
of a joint are laid alongside each other on their
backs or rind surface; glue is applied quickly to all
at once by a few rapid strokes of a wide brush; the
strips are brought together and the joint is held at
both ends in a lathe; while one worker turns the
joint by the lathe handle, another winds it with
tape, in overlapping spirals.   A hand-rest extends
along the front of the lathe.   After winding, the
joints are hung up by the small end to dry and
season, being suspended by means of little clamps.

ROD-MAKING:

FERRULES AND THEIR FITTING; ONE-PIECE AND SPLICED RODS

CHAPTER VII

ROD-MAKING:
FERRULES AND THEIR FITTING;
ONE-PIECE AND SPLICED RODS

Rod ferrules, the metal tubular fittings attached to the ends of rod-joints, by means of which the rod is jointed up or assembled for use, are made preferably of German-silver (white-metal) or of gun-metal. Many high-grade English rods are made up with the gun-metal ferrules, reel-seat, etc., and in this dead black finish they are both very suitable and elegant. It would be somewhat difficult to obtain these latter from domestic tackle-dealers; possibly they might be supplied to special order through some of the more prominent anglers' supply-houses. Handmade German-silver ferrules are readily obtained on special order, the price [7] being from one to two dollars a pair and may include waterproofing and serration. Stock ferrules in this metal are kept by all of the larger tackle-dealers, the variety and grade of some being much better than those of others. With the best of these available, the writer would

[7] The prices that we have noted for all rod-fittings are " before-the-war " quotations, and current prices are so unstable that we have let these stand. From thirty to fifty per-cent advance must be allowed, and more on some things. The agate used for guides formerly was imported principally from Austria.

deem the handmade article a luxury except for the very practical advantage of being able to obtain them in any diameter desired, exactly gauged to one-thousandth of an inch. The reader interested in exceptionally high-class rod-accessories, will do well to consult John G. Landman, 59 Cedar Street, Brooklyn, New York. Edward vom Hofe and Co. also manufacture certain fittings on their own premises, at 112 Fulton Street, New York; and we have found Ogilvie's, at 79 Chambers Street, New York, very satisfactory for some things. Ferrules carried in stock may be bought at prices ranging from fifteen to seventy-five cents per pair, according to size and style.

The British taste in ferrules tends strongly to those furnished with some sort of locking device — "lockfast" joints. These are made abroad in great variety, but to American eyes they seem cumbersome, unsightly, and altogether unnecessary. The plain American, friction (suction or vacuum) ferrule, depending for its holding power wholly upon mechanically exact fitting, looks pretty good to the American angler, who never has had legitimate cause to worry about any tendency in it to throw apart.

Ferrules come in pairs consisting of the male (center or inner) ferrule and the female (outer or receiving) half, the outside diameter of a male ferrule being identical with the inside measurement of its mating section. Either the male or female ferrules may be purchased separately. This is a convenience, especially in the case of male ferrules, because of the customary duplication of the top-joints of rods, for the purpose of having one in reserve against a smash-up. The male ferrule is attached to the butt or larger end of a rod-joint.

As ferrules constitute rigid portions of the rod, which otherwise is uniformly flexible from butt to tip, it is evident that *it is a mistake to have them any longer than is necessary for efficient service.* For rods eight to ten feet in length, a union of one and one-eighth to one and one-quarter inches — depth of penetration of male ferrule — is sufficient at the joint between the butt- and middle-sections of the rod, and of three-quarters to an inch between the middle-joint and top. This will give a desirable over-all length of at least about two and one-half inches for the larger female ferrule of a ten-foot rod.

Waterproof ferrules are supplied at an extra cost; they are made by soldering a disk of metal within the female ferrule at the point where it is intended that this partition shall come down against the end of the rod-joint, in order to prevent access of water to the otherwise unprotected wood here; and wood absorbs moisture more rapidly from the ends than from the sides, and especially at these bamboo-ends unprotected by enamel. However, neither does the author consider these are a necessity, as he is willing to take the risk of any water finding its way into the joint of a rod that is fitted with ordinary ferrules set on after the manner which will be recommended.

Ferrules are cataloged as plain straight; shouldered, capped or swelled; straight with rim or welt;

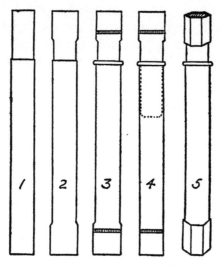

Varieties of ferrules: (1) Plain straight; (2) Shouldered, swelled or capped; (3) Capped with rim welt; 4) Straight with welt, and capped and closed center; (5) Hexagonal ends

and shouldered with welt. And some have hexagonal proximal or rod-joint ends — which do not appeal strongly to the majority of experienced anglers. The accompanying illustrations show exactly what is understood by the above terms. The kind here recommended (number 4 in the illustration) has a straight-sided female member, and a shouldered male member that is closed at the distal end —" closed-end center." They are obtainable from Abbey and Imbrie, at 97 Chambers Street, New York City, under the name of " bamboo " ferrules. We also have obtained similar satisfactory ferrules from the T. H. Chubb Rod Co., of Post Mills, Vermont, which that firm catalogs as their " special short, straight, welted ferrule, with capped and closed-end center." The Abbey and Imbrie ferrules, at the time of this writing, were supplied in the following sizes, the figures denoting in fractions of an inch the outside diameter of the male or inside diameter of the female or outer member: $\frac{9}{64}$, $\frac{11}{64}$, $\frac{3}{16}$, $\frac{7}{32}$, $\frac{15}{64}$, $\frac{1}{4}$, $\frac{17}{64}$, $\frac{19}{64}$, $\frac{11}{32}$, $\frac{3}{8}$, $\frac{27}{64}$, $\frac{15}{32}$, $\frac{1}{2}$, $\frac{35}{64}$, $\frac{19}{32}$, $\frac{5}{8}$, $\frac{43}{64}$, $\frac{23}{32}$, $\frac{3}{4}$, $\frac{51}{64}$, $\frac{55}{64}$, $\frac{7}{8}$, $\frac{61}{64}$, $\frac{63}{64}$, $1\frac{1}{32}$. The Chubb article ran in somewhat different sizes, namely: $\frac{5}{32}$, $\frac{3}{16}$, $\frac{13}{64}$, $\frac{15}{64}$, $\frac{17}{64}$, $\frac{19}{64}$, $\frac{11}{32}$, $\frac{3}{8}$, $\frac{13}{32}$, $\frac{7}{16}$, $\frac{15}{32}$, $\frac{17}{32}$, $\frac{19}{32}$, $\frac{5}{8}$, $\frac{11}{16}$, $\frac{23}{32}$, $\frac{13}{16}$. Once again the reader is cautioned that he should be prepared to find that actual *diameters of stock ferrules may vary* minutely from the sizes as listed.

The sizes used by the writer for the ten-foot fly, nine- and nine and one-half-foot fly, and five and one-quarter-foot bait-casting rods mentioned in a previous chapter, are respectively $2\frac{1}{46}$ and $\frac{13}{64}$ inch; $\frac{9}{32}$ and $\frac{11}{64}$; and $\frac{19}{64}$ inch. For the independent-hand-grasp joint, for the fly-rods, $\frac{7}{16}$ and $\frac{3}{8}$ inch.

Ferrules that are a *trifle* large should be selected,

rather than those a bit undersized for the joint at the place where they are to be fitted — when compelled to make the choice — as but a minimum amount of the wood should be cut away, *especially in fitting the female ferrules,* which preferably are without a shoulder, as already noted. The ferrule diameter should on no account be *materially less than the rod diameter* as measured, this time, between *flat surfaces,* at the meeting ends of the rod-joints where the ferrule is to be used; hence calipering these ends in this way will inform you of the ferrule sizes required. An expedient sometimes of value when fitting to old joints new ferrules that are a trifle large, is to wind the joint-ends with waxed silk or fine linen-thread before applying the cement, and then to force the ferrules on over this.

Only ferrules whose parts fit snugly together should be accepted and used. If too tight, the male ferrule is easily dressed down by turning it, together with its attached rod-joint, inside of a folded piece of fine emery-cloth held tightly between the fingers, finishing the process by rubbing it with a mixture of powdered chalk and linseed oil. *Never use a file for this purpose.*

The proximal ends of ferrules — ends toward the rod-joints — should be either *split or serrated* for a short distance, in order to modify rigidity here. If this be not done, there are created abrupt lines of demarkation around the rod at every point where

the flexible bamboo emerges from
the rigid metal tubing; and it is at
one of these places that the rod is
most likely to give way under excep-
tional stress. A further good expedient to relieve the strain at joint
connections, is to *locate a line-guide
at the lower end of each female ferrule,* so that the line pull at these
ferrule guides will come more directly against the stronger side of
the joints between the separate
pieces of the rod.

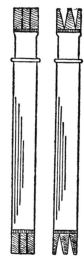

Split and serrated
ferrules

The amateur rod-tinker need not
however pay the dealer the very
considerable cost of ferrules hav-
ing flexible ends — fifty or seventy-five cents more
a pair — but, with the use either of a fine hack-saw
or a small triangular saw-file, he may proceed to do
his own splitting or serrating, as the case may be.
When using the saw, it is advisable first to fit a plug
of soft wood snugly within the ferrule-end to be
sawed and to cut it off flush with the metal. In

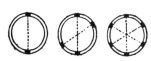

Figures 1, 2, and 3 — Guiding-
notches for serrating ferrules

using the file, first notch the
ferrule-end in two places,
corresponding to its exact
middle diameter, by one
stroke of the tool held hori-
zontally (Fig. 1). Next, divide each half of the

circle, by notches, equally into three arcs, by two additional file-strokes (Figures 2 and 3). You now

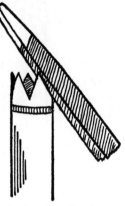

have made your six guiding-notches with but three strokes. Deepen these notches a little, and then be sure to *equalize them, by directing the side pressure of the file* as required, before completing the cutting to the full depth. For this the file now is held in an inclined position, as the illustration depicts, and you make short strokes away from you.

Serrating ferrules

For securing the ferrules in the vise without injury while sawing slits or filing notches, make a little holder from two pieces of soft wood, by chiseling a V-groove along a side of each, as represented in Fig. 4.

Fig. 4 — Wooden ferrule-holder

Several kinds of preparations are in use for cementing the ferrules onto the rod-joints, among them being common thick shellac, sealing-wax, bicycle-tire and gutta-percha dental cements. As an excellent and inexpensive ready-prepared article may be had in the shops, we never have bothered about cement recipes; the author uses Dodge's ferrule cement, which he buys at William Mills and Son's, 21 Park Place, New York City, for twenty-five cents a stick — enough to last a long time. Doubtless it may be obtained in many places, or a similar preparation that will serve as well. Whatever else you do in securing the ferrules to the wood, do *not* make use of any metal pins; they weaken the rod, are no effective preventive against loosening, and they constitute an annoying obstruction when the re-cementing of a ferrule is indicated. And do not use doweled ferrules.

In fitting your ferrules, be sure that the female section is not thrust too far down over its joint-end, and so *prevents the male ferrule from being seated the full depth;* by placing the smaller (seating) part of the male ferrule alongside the outer end of the female, measure the distance down on the joint that the bottom of the female ferrule should extend, and

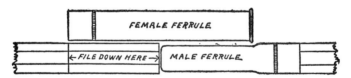

Finding point on joint for bottom edge of female ferrule

mark this point on the wood. Allow for the least bit of space between the wood end within the female ferrule and the butt end of the male, when the rod is jointed up. Cut the wood down by careful cross-filing — as you roll the end of the joint on the workbench, followed by turning it within a fold of sandpaper — only sufficient for a good snug fit of metal over the wood; and remember that the ferrule will expand a bit when heated. Be especially careful to *have the female ferrule fit the wood as tightly as possible,* for it is this ferrule that is more likely to work loose from its attachment. As you file and sandpaper, pause now and then to try on the ferrule, giving to it a twisting motion, which will leave black rubbing-marks on the wood that indicate the high spots requiring further cutting away.

In your filing of the joint, endeavor to remove the wood *equally on all sides,* in order that the ferrules will be *centered,* and thus bring the whole rod into true alignment when its sections are jointed together.

In applying the cement, be careful to avoid getting any upon that inside part of the outer ferrule which receives the male (inner) section. Soften the stick of cement in the flame of an alcohol lamp, a gas- or candle-flame; stick a few small gobs on the wood, and heat the cement and joint-end over the flame carefully, turning the joint to and fro the while, till the cement flows; spread the now liquefied cement evenly over the wood by stroking lengthwise with a match, toothpick, or sliver of bamboo; slip the ferrule on as far as it readily will go; heat ferrule and all again *over* the flame a moment, then by firmly pushing against the floor or some other solid object, as the door-jamb, quickly force the ferrule home to your mark. The excess of cement exuding from between the ferrule-end and the wood is best removed while yet hot and semi-liquid, by a circular wiping stroke with a rag, or better, by turning the joint against the rag; and when cold and hard, it easily is chipped off with a knife-blade manipulated cautiously.

As German-silver ferrules are *tempered, overheating directly in a flame is injurious to the metal.*

File down paper-thin the extreme ends of the teeth made in serrating, as the silk-winding is to extend up over them onto the solid metal; and, to make a " very particular job," you also may file down the whole length of the outside surface of the teeth or slit portions to just beyond their bases, so that the silk-wrapping, at its termination on the ferrule, will lie nearly or quite flush with the metal surface it butts against. The shaded portions of the illustrations of serrated and split ferrules represent this area of superficial filing. One of the teeth or sections between slits will lie against each flat surface of the 1od-joint, except that in the case of the smaller-top ferrules you may make but three serrations and have a tooth lie along each alternate flat face of the rod.

As a precaution against dampness, you may varnish the extreme joint-ends, which receive the female ferrules, before attaching the ferrules, and then when applying the cement to the joint you also can spread a smooth coating of this over the same place.

There are yet other devices. Mr. W. L. Ayles-worth, an English authority, states that paraffine or type-metal is much more penetrating than either var-nish, shellac, or most any other coating compound, and that if the paraffine be melted, the ferrule heated, and the paraffine poured into the ferrule onto the bare wood, it will penetrate for a considerable dis-tance and renders it absolutely waterproof. A warmed glass medicine-dropper is a handy tool with which to introduce your paraffine.

Mr. Aylesworth further remarks: " In fact, it is difficult to say which is the better compound, for both are very penetrating and satisfactory for this purpose. The neglect to waterproof wood at the fer-

Sealing and locking ferrules with type-metal

rules and protect it from moisture probably has more to do with the joints breaking at these places than the angler is aware of. It also is a good plan to turn or file a small groove around the joint, at about an eighth of an inch from the end entering the female ferrule, and to turn the end down slightly so that the type-metal, if used, will run down between the wood and the ferrule and into the groove. This will have a tendency to solder the ferrule onto the wood. Melt the type-metal in a spoon or ladle and pour it in the ferrule on the wood after cementing, by use of a small funnel."

The present writer prefers to rely for fixation of ferrules wholly upon snug fitting and cement, and he uses the paraffine for waterproofing the bare wood at the joint-ends.

When all your ferrules are fitted, you can make some little wooden plugs for the open ends of the female ferrules, both to guard them against injury and to keep out dirt and dust.   Stock ferrules are not supplied with any sealing device, but handmade ferrules may have little caps (grease-caps) that fit snugly within their ends, and which may be slightly greased or oiled before inserting, when the rod is disjointed.

Wood ferrule-plug

One-Piece and Spliced Rods.—In the endeavor wholly to obviate this rigid feature of metal ferrule connections in rod construction, some rods — especially veteran salmon-rods of English, Scotch, or Irish manufacture, are without ferrules of any kind, being made to joint up by a whipped splice; or again, rods are made, even up to eleven feet long, in one clear length of split-bamboo — one-piece or one-joint rods.   You rarely see today a rod of either description, and almost never in America, as any slight advantage of such construction is not at all commensurate either with the greatly-increased difficulty of building and the consequent extremely high cost, or with the inconvenience entailed in the transportation of or in the putting-up and taking-down of the rod. A ferruled rod, built with the precautions that have been noted, is good enough for the most fastidious angler; beyond a certain point, additional refinements belong within the category of the exquisite rather than the useful.

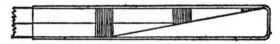

Spliced-rod joint-end and cap

The manner of jointing the spliced rod may be of interest to the reader. The splicing ends of the joints have long bevels, of several inches; these are reinforced by fine silk-whippings, and may be protected when the rod is not in use by metal caps which slip over them. Before splicing the joints in the preparation of the rod for use, warmed shoemakers'-wax or beeswax is thoroughly applied both to the beveled surfaces of the wood and to the linen-

Spliced-rod lashing

thread which binds the splice together. In addition to the circular turns of this wrapping-thread, lashings running lengthwise under the former are sometimes used, which pass through little metal rings or around hooks for further security against the joints throwing apart.   (Our diagrammatic sketch shows the splice rather short.)

ROD-MAKING:
WINDINGS AND GUIDES

.

CHAPTER VIII

ROD-MAKING: WINDINGS AND GUIDES

The silk windings (wrappings or whippings) of a split-bamboo rod, in addition to securing the line-guides in position and serving as a most effective reinforcing bond for holding together the individual strips of which each rod-joint is composed, are generally considered a factor in adding to the rigidity of the rod. In commercial practise the joints are held in a lathe-like apparatus while being wound, but this is not at all necessary for the limited operations of the amateur. Authorities on practical angling nearly all believe that closer winding will stiffen a rod appreciably. From this it might be inferred that a rod solidly wound throughout its whole length would be very much stiffened; however, solid winding does not work out this way in practise, making the rod logy rather, and it is not in favor with experienced rod connoisseurs. In fact, some of the very finest modern rods have no windings except those that attach the guides and overlap the ferrules.

As already has been mentioned, the writer regards silk windings as very much superior to any form of metal wrappings; but, when he uses them at all except for guide lashings, he applies the silk — differently from the usual method of a series of individual, narrow circular bands — in the form of a continuous trellised or diamond-patterned whipping which extends the whole length of the joints. And he whips with unwaxed silk, just as obtained from the drygoods store. For this method he claims the following very practical advantages, wholly irrespective of its highly distinctive appearance: It makes a good holding-ground for the varnish, the bare outer skin of bamboo offering, in this respect, a surface not much more acceptable than does glass or steel; it supports or stiffens the rod to a greater degree than could the closest practical individual bands, a good idea of its effectiveness being obtained by comparing the " backbone " of a top-joint thus wound — and even before any varnish is applied — with its unwound duplicate; it materially assists in preventing set; it reduces to a minimum the number of invisible-end fastenings necessitated in the complete winding of the rod.

Unwaxed silk is preferred as offering the varnish a better chance to penetrate, shrink it, and glue it down onto the wood. And we do not use the more brittle white shellac, white French lacquer, or thin white glue or mucilage as a preliminary coating for the windings, to prevent a darkening of the silk, which we do not regard as at all objectionable.

(Equal parts of collodion and banana oil is used for the same purpose.) On the other hand, if the proper colors and shades of silk be selected, our personal taste approves this increased depth of color as imparting a less flashy, richer, and altogether more elegant appearance. But restrain your preference from running to delicate, weakly-defined shades, as you will be unpleasantly surprised to see how they will lose character under the effect of varnish. If you do not want the diamond whipping to contrast with the color of the bamboo, select for this a light orange or a yellow shade and it will be almost invisible except on close inspection. If you do use white shellac in alcohol for the primary coat, to preserve the original shade of the silk, make but the thinnest application of it.

The most satisfactory colors for windings are black, a bright green or red, yellow, a good brown, or purple — neither of the latter in too dark a shade and all these used either in one solid color or in various combinations. Yellow and red, yellow and green, or green and black are good used together.

We employ the size A silk, commonly used in millinery and dressmaking, and thus readily obtainable at any drygoods " emporium." This is about the thickness of what the tackle-dealers grade as medium or coarse; for the finer silk-thread in colors you must apply either to them or to jobbers in the trade, as you will not find it on general sale, though perchance on occasion at the " art-embroidery " counter of one of the larger department-stores. To be sure, you can.split the A silk and make use of only a part of its strands; this, however, hardly without waxing. But if your ideal in rods is represented by a good service-able article, not much under five ounces in weight, the A size is none too heavy. Rods are made much lighter than this and they are very exquisite; and may be very efficient, too — *for the expert under the usual conditions prevailing in the smaller streams.* Yet we have seen a sixteen-inch brown trout, *Salmo fario,* in a four-foot-wide stretch of water; and even though the size of the fish in the small streams may average seven to nine inches in length, the fisherman never knows when that whopper will grab his fly, nor in what difficult situation he may be obliged to con-trol him promptly if the prize is to be creeled — and where is the angler who would not gladly sacri-fice all his smaller catch rather than *lose that chance big fellow?*

The brands of silk-thread found usually in the stores are either the Corticelli, Belding, or Heming-way. We have no choice, but can indicate by the numbers stamped on the respective spools the shades in the Hemingway brand that will work out effec-tively. These are: purple, number 794 — or very dark, 1044; brown, number 484; green, 891; and red, 633. There is a shade of green in the Corticelli brand very like the Hemingway 891, but having a yellower glint, that is a bit better.

Start the continuous winding at the butt-end of the rod-joint, by making a few circular turns of the silk away from you; the end is caught beneath these initial turns (Fig. 1), and wetting the end of the

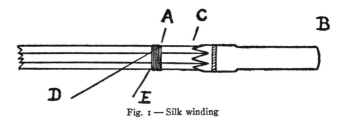

Fig. 1 — Silk winding

silk will prevent it from slipping when you commence. You now are holding the joint in your left hand and its butt or male-ferrule end is directed to the right. To ascertain the exact point of starting, A, you must measure off from the joint-end, B, a sufficient distance nicely to clear the other end of the ferrule, at C, as *the ferrule winding is to be a separate affair.*

Next, turn the joint butt-end to your left; hold the circular turns with your left thumb while cutting off short the silk-end, D, with a *sharp* knife; and start to wind a spiral toward the smaller end, rotating the joint away from you between the fingers of the left hand, while you hold the silk (E) taut between the thumb and forefinger of the right hand,

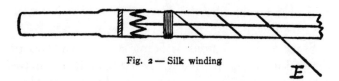

Fig. 2 — Silk winding

pulling toward you and to the right (Fig. 2). The spool-end, E, is rendering from the spool as you hold the latter in your hand, or as it rests in a convenient receptacle to prevent its rolling away.

The symmetrically-graduated spacing of this first spiral-winding is guided entirely by the eye. For butt-joints, the writer starts the turns spaced from three-quarters to five-eighths of an inch, and gradually runs them down to one-half inch apart at the smaller end; on middle-joints, the turns are spaced one-half inch at butt, gradually diminishing to one-quarter inch; and for the top-joint, they run from one-quarter inch down to one-eighth inch at the rod's tip. On the *butt-joint he lays up three courses of windings to each spiral, side by side, two courses similarly on the middle- and a single-thread course on the top-joint.*

To know when to terminate the spiral-windings at the female-ferrule end of the joint, you previously

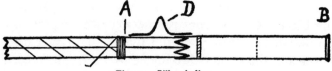

Fig. 3 — Silk winding

must have noted the spot (A, Fig. 3) by a pencil-
mark, after measuring from the ferrule-end, B, a
sufficient distance both to clear the ferrule and to
allow space for the line-guide, D, that is to be located
here.   End the spiral by a few close turns at A;
then turn the joint so that the end B is again directed
to your left, and start the return spiral.   For all
spiral-windings *returning over the same course* you
must reverse your *thread* by looping it and catching

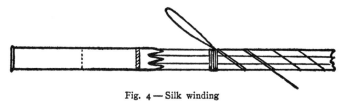

Fig. 4 — Silk winding

the loop with a few circular turns that are cast over
it, as illustrated in Fig. 4.   Do not mind any bunch-
ing of circular turns here, as both the loops and these
circular turns are but temporary, and all will be *cut
away later, when a smooth, permanent circular-
winding takes their place.*   This looping maneuver
is necessitated in laying the second and third courses
of each spiral-winding on butt-joints, and for the
second course on middle-joints.   To produce the
diamond-whipping on top-joints, in single-thread
spirals, it is not necessary; you then continue to wind
ahead without reversing the *thread,* till the four
spirals are finished, simply by crossing your thread

— after completing one circular turn which termi-
nates each spiral course — and by reversing the
joint, end for end, which starts you back all right
when a succeeding spiral is to be wound in the same
direction *around* the joint, but *lengthwise* of the
joint in a direction opposite to that taken by its immediate predecessor. Complex as this may sound,
it really is the acme of simplicity in operation, as
you will learn at the very first attempt.

In order to have the spacing of the second spiral
conform to that of the one first wound, it is necessary only to see that the threads of the two spirals

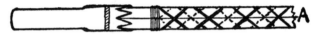

Fig. 5 — Silk winding

cross at the same angular side of the rod-joint,
which you select in preference to a flat surface, for
more accurate guidance (A, Fig. 5).

Two additional spirals are needed to produce the
closer trellised or diamond effect sought, and these
are laid so as to halve the space (as shown by the
dotted lines in the illustration) between the spirals
previously wound, the eye alone readily serving here
as an efficient guide.

Intricate as the process may appear from the ultimate result, the reader soon will understand that it
is only the first spirals over each joint that must be
wound with a great deliberation and care as to sym-

metrically-graduated spacing.   That does determine
the outcome, but the subsequent spirals are wound
with increasing rapidity.   Attention is directed also
to the fact that even the most serious mishap to any
part of the continuous winding, after the rod is completed, *in no case necessitates rewinding the whole
joint,* but only of the short interval between two consecutive solid windings, whether guide- or ferrule-
wrappings.

All rod-windings are terminated finally by an " in-
visible-knot " ending.   Before taking up the question of guide- and ferrule-wrappings and their location on the rod — the detailed layout — we will
describe several ways of making the invisible knot or
whip finish, which, after all, attain but one and the
same result.   The winder soon will find that the
particular method which is most convenient will de-
pend both on himself and on the particular location
of a winding, or on other special conditions under
which he is compelled to make the fastening.   The
mystery of this is the chief secret of rod-winding,
and it really is no " knot " at all, but a trick of
burying the end under the final turns in order at once
to get it out of the way and to keep the winding
from unwrapping.

The illustrations that follow, Figures 1 to 9, show
windings made with a coarse thread instead of the
actual winding-silk, for the purpose of clearer delin-
eation.

We start a solid circular-winding in exactly the same way that we started the spiral-winding, that is by catching the starting-end of the thread under the first few coils.   When nearing the end of your wrapping, hold the last tight coil, A, with the thumb of

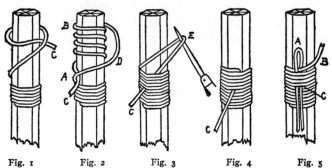

Fig. 1   Fig. 2   Fig. 3   Fig. 4   Fig. 5

Silk winding: (1) Starting the loose coils; (2) Free end of silk run under; (3) Loose coils wound tightly over terminal end — awl-point holds loop; (4) The loop drawn in; (5) Separate-loop method

the left hand, while — after cutting the silk to allow a sufficiently long end — with the other hand you make several *loose coils,* B, in the same direction around the joint as previously, but a short distance from and winding back toward this last tight coil; insert the free end of the silk, C, under the coil, A, held by the left thumb; continue the winding by holding on to the loop, D, which unwraps the loose coils while at the same time it transfers them into tight coils laid up against the completed section of the permanent winding and binds the terminal silk-end tightly underneath; insert a large pin, point of a finishing-nail, or any similar pointed instrument (a shoemakers'-awl is most handy for this) through the loop, E, which holds it taut to prevent it from kinking, then draw the loop up close to this, drop or pull out the pin (or whatever your bodkin may be), and at the same instant quickly pull the end, C, up tight; cut off the surplus free end close to where it emerges from the wrapping, with a quick sawing motion of a *sharp* knife.

A modification of the above method makes use of a separate loop of heavy, waxed linen-thread, for the purpose of pulling the terminal silk-end under the last few coils, which already have been wound tight. The loop (A, Fig. 5) is laid in place lengthwise of the rod-joint as you approach the end of a wrapping, several coils are carried over it, and then the free end of the winding-thread, B, is pushed through the loop and pulled under and out, where the loop emerges at C. In using very fine winding-silk, a fine needle may be substituted for the loop, and the end of the thread inserted through its eye.

Another method, that the author frequently adopts, consists in making the final loose turns both over joint and the tapered end of a miniature.marlin-pin or a lead-pencil point laid alongside of the joint. The end then is turned back through these coils, between the marlin-pin and the joint, as Fig. 6 depicts; the forefinger of the left hand holds the last tight coil against the joint as the marlin-pin is withdrawn.

The first loose coil, B, then is picked up by inserting under it the point of the shoemakers'-awl; the thread-end, C, is caught by tightening this coil, and the remaining loose coils are laid up against the rest of the wrapping, which is completed in the same manner as described above.

The most ingenious method of all, but not always applicable, is first to decide under how many coils you wish to bury the terminal-end, and then to throw

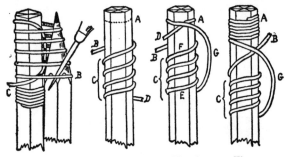

Fig. 6   Fig. 7   Fig. 8   Fig. 9
Silk winding: (6) Marlin-pin method; (7,8, and 9) Method in which terminal coils are thrown first around joint

these coils loosely around the joint upon *beginning* the wrapping. The silk is not cut until all is finished and pulled taut, so none is wasted. It practically is a reversal of the method first described. Referring to Fig. 7, suppose that it is desired to start at A and to wind toward the bottom of the page. B is the spool-end of the silk, C indicates four loose coils, and D is the loose-end of the silk. The first step is to catch the end, D, under the first turn of the wrapping, as shown in Fig. 8. You now can wind ahead, holding the silk at G and rotating the joint to the left, as far as you like. As the F-end of the loose coils is renewed from the spool as fast as the E-end unwinds, these four coils are carried right along throughout the whole wrapping. When ready to end the winding, passing the spool-end of the silk, B (spool and all), under the winding-thread, G, catches it as shown in Fig. 9. Continue the wrapping to dispose of the four loose coils, pull the end (B) taut, cut it short, and your wrapping is completed.

A hexagonal lead-pencil and a piece of ordinary wrapping-twine are good materials with which to practise the details of these windings and endings.

When making solid wrappings, press all the coils firmly together from time to time, with some suitable blunt instrument, as the edge of a paper-cutter or back of a table-knife; and when completed, before varnishing, rub them smooth with the rounding handle of a tooth-brush — all the better if it is of the old-time genuine bone variety. Also at this time you may apply a match- or candle-flame *for an instant* to any fuzz or thread-ends that may be projecting in an unsightly fashion; but an alcohol flame is the best, being less likely to smudge light-colored silk. You readily can detect these ends by sighting lengthwise along the joint, as you slowly rotate it.

We are assuming, now, that all ferrules have been serrated or split and are cemented in position, that the diamond-whipping is in place, and that a preliminary thin coat of varnish has been applied to the joint and is dry. We have yet to bind on the line-guides and to put on the ferrule-wrappings. This is done with individual close-laid or solid circular-windings, and they constitute *all of the windings of this character that are needed on any rod-joints that previously have been wound as we have described.*

Naturally, we first must determine how many guides we shall use and just where they shall be

Guide and winding layout for 10-foot fly-rod

located; also whether these solid wrappings shall be of the same color as the diamond-winding or of a contrasting color. To the writer's taste, all-green windings, yellow touched off with red or green, or green touched with black make a strong appeal. Let us suppose that we have agreed upon the latter, and that we now are at work on the ten-foot fly-rod. Our winding-plan would be as shown in the accompanying diagram, the figures indicating the distances in inches from guide-center to guide-center, when the rod is assembled. The darker windings are those of the black silk, and these, beginning with the three bands grouped at the rod-butt, which are a scant one-eighth inch wide, should gradually diminish in width all the way to the rod's tip, where they may consist of only four or five turns of thread. When making top-joints in duplicate or triplicate, it is a good plan to distinguish them by special arrangements of bands at their tips; you then can always identify the particular one in use.

After the positions of the guides are located, bands of black silk are wound around the joint, over the spiral-winding at each point where the guide-wrapping will come, and in such a way that each solid guide-wrapping of green will be set off at its ends with a narrow black border. When once these are in place, and in addition to the rest of the joint have had their *preliminary coat of varnish to hold the silk here, the spiral-winding is cut and unwound between them at each guide-site;* the guides then are bound on close against the wood, when their wrappings may receive a first coat of varnish.

Note that a guide is placed at each ferrule-connection, at its lower and stronger side. Some further detail is called for concerning the guide-windings at the ferrules and the ferrule-windings themselves, and reference to the accompanying diagram will materially aid in understanding about this. Before starting to wind on a guide at the end of a joint or to wrap a ferrule, first we place a smooth, permanent circular-wrapping (A) alongside and below the lumpy, temporary circular turns at the ends of the diamong-whipping; *we then cut away these unsightly coils of the first or spiral winding that were necessitated in applying it.* We now have a clear space from A to E, and we use the length of the guide (C), which is to be located here, as a measure for the exact extent of this space.

All guides are wound *solidly* from end to end — that is, the winding extends underneath the ele-

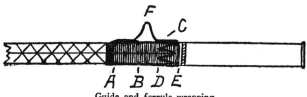

Guide and ferrule wrapping

vated part of the guide; and the wrappings at the ferrules *cover in the serrated ends up to and lapping the solid metal, at E, to prevent access of water or dampness at that end of the ferrule.* From A to E the winding consists of *three sections.* It is started at D — the point on the rod-joint where the shank or foot of the guide meets its standing part; then is carried to B, when the guide is placed in position and its proximal (lower or inner) shank is covered in, from B to A; and it ends with its last coil close up against the band at A. The other shank (distal, upper or outer foot) of the guide, C, *overlaps about half-way the ferrule-tooth* that lies on the flat surface of the joint to which the guide is applied. The ends both of this shank of the guide and of the ferrule-tooth have previously been filed down thin with the little saw-file. The wrapping is completed by the wholly *independent section* represented by D — E, starting at D; thus *this section alone must be removed for the purpose of re-cementing a loosened female-ferrule,* and the guide is not disturbed in its position.

Before securing any guides to the rod, it is most important that it should experimentally have been jointed up with different flat surfaces of its respective sections in alignment, in order *to determine what particular arrangement gives the best results;* and when this has been accomplished you should *mark the guide surfaces* of each joint for future identification. However carefully you have endeavored to center the ferrules on the joints, you probably will be surprised to find when the rod is jointed up in certain ways that there will be produced quite a decided angular deflection at least at one of the junctions, but which a slight rotation of one of the connecting pieces may correct. If not satisfactorily remedied in this way, then joint the two rod-sections together in their best position and hold the union — both including ferrules and the wood within them — over the alcohol-lamp flame, heat all very carefully but thoroughly, and then very cautious but firm manipulation between the hands — one at either side of the ferrule-joint with thumbs extended — will solve the difficulty.

With due regard to what has been said above, you should try also to have any rod-joint which may show a slight long bend extending throughout its whole length, so placed that the flat side most identified with the convexity shall be the down or guide side when the rod is held in position of use — with reel underneath, for the fly-rod. In other words, the guides should line up when the rod-sections are jointed in the best possible position, looking to the truest alignment and best action of the whole rod.

It now remains to consider the guides themselves; what kind shall we use?

For both bottom- and tip-guides — points of greatest friction — we should select appropriate agate or phosphor-bronze guides; and some pretty good imitation-agate guides have been marketed, at a material reduction in cost from the price of the genuine. Very satisfactory, and by not a few anglers preferred even to agate, is what is known as the " Perfection " tip-guide; it is made in Denver, by the Perfection Tip Co., of file-proof tungsten steel with German-silver tube. It is light, neat, and practically indestructible and frictionless. It costs fifty cents.

18.   17   16
4/64   5/64   6/64

Agate angle fly tip-
guides

The same concern makes also of similar material splendidly efficient and durable butt-guides, and reel-guides that may be attached to a cross-bar. For the other (intermediate) guides on your fly-rod you want a standing form of guide that is called the " snake " guide, and these to be of steel and not of German-silver, which latter soon is grooved by the friction of the line. Snake-guides were once an English innovation but long have ceased to be a novelty, being almost univer-

" Perfection "   steel tip-guide for fly-rod (enlarged)

sally used today on all makes of the highest-class rods; both in appearance and utility they are a great advance over the old ring-and-keeper de-

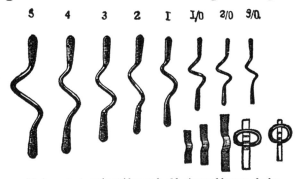

5   4   3   2   1   1/0   2/0   3/0

Modern steel snake-guides and old ring-and-keeper device

vice. The line is not so likely to foul them, and it renders much more freely through them, so that the cast as well as the length of life of the line both are thereby influenced favorably. There is one remaining convenient use for the ring with keeper — that is to attach one at the butt of your rod just above the handgrasp, *to hook your fly into when not in use.*

Our illustration shows how these snake-guides are numbered according to their gradation in size, from 3/0 up to 5. They may be purchased from almost any tackle-house for about twenty cents a dozen.

9   10   11   12

Agate (German-silver mounted) light "Tournament" casting-guide

Reference to a previous illustration, "Guide and winding layout," will show that the fly-rods of nine feet and over carry twelve of these guides; and from butt to tip we use them in this order and in about these sizes: 4, 3, 2, 2, 2, 1, 1, 1/0, 1/0, 2/0, 2/0, 3/0. For eight-foot rods, use two guides less and space them as follows, beginning at the butt-end: Bottom-guide is 17¼ inches from butt of rod; from its center to center of bottom intermediate-guide, 9½ inches; next space, 9 inches; then 8½, 7½, 7¼, 6¾, 6½, 6⅛, 5⅝, 5, and 4½ inches respectively.

For the bottom-guide on the fly-rod, the author uses the light " Tournament " agate-guide, as pictured, which vom Hofe cataloged as size number 10, and which used to cost thirty-five cents (there was a smaller size, number 9); and for the agate tip-guide, vom Hofe's tubular form, $\frac{5}{64}$ inch in diameter, costing thirty cents.[8]

Another neat English device is an agate angle tip-guide, with two legs, made to wind on instead of to be cemented.

English agate angle fly tip-guide for winding on

Abbey and Imbrie, 97 Chambers, New York, have carried these, at fifty cents. The same firm had also a similar device in a larger size, but all in bronze, the guide-ring turning within its encircling wire loop, which they sold for forty cents; they are nice for mounting bait- or trolling-tops.

For the short, bait-casting rod, we have adopted the layout shown below (Fig. 1), all of the guides being attached to the top-joint.

Fig. 1 — Guide layout for short, bait-casting rod

The bottom-guide is of the same style as that selected for the fly-rod, but in the larger size, number 12.   The agate tip-

8 We note again that all these are pre-war prices.

Agate   "Western"   casting
tip-guide

guide is vom Hofe's "Western offset" style, $\frac{7}{64}$ inch in diameter (number 2/0), priced at forty cents. The same size in the "Dowagiac" pattern was sold at thirty-five cents. The two intermediate guides are the same maker's "Improved" or one-ring casting style, numbers 1 and 0 respectively; price nine cents each. Abbey and Imbrie used to stock phosphor-bronze revolving-center

| 4/0 | 3/0 | 2/0 | 1/0 | 1 |
| 7/64 | 8/64 | 9/64 | 10/64 | 12/64 in |

"Dowagiac" pattern agate casting tip-guide

guides mounted like these one-ring casting-guides; the idea of the revolving-center feature is that the line will draw equally against all sides of the ring and so will eliminate grooving. They are quite as effective as agate-guides and much less liable to breakage.

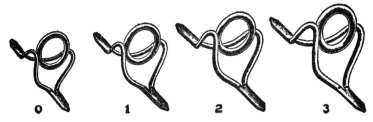

German-silver "Improved" one-ring casting-guide

Some anglers would prefer to locate the bottom-guide of the bait-casting rod a few inches ahead of the ferrule, rather than at the ferrule as shown in Fig. 1 above; and they would use only one intermediate guide between that and the tip, placing but three guides on this rod, in all.

Agate stirrup-pattern casting tip-guide

In order to permit equalization of the strain on two sides of the top-joint, the guides may be attached in pairs, after the usual manner employed in the heavier, surf-casting rods (Fig. 2); in this case the tip-guide should not be offset but

Fig. 2 — Paired guides

should be one of center alignment, stirrup pattern, as shown. Abbey and Imbrie sell it, size number 3½, for sixty-five cents, in agate; in imitation agate, thirty-five cents.

ROD-MAKING:

HANDGRASP AND REELSEAT

CHAPTER IX

ROD-MAKING: HANDGRASP AND REELSEAT

The handle of a rod is termed the handgrasp. It preferably is made of superimposed perforated disks of solid cork, cemented together and upon a common core, and then trimmed to shape and smoothed up with sandpaper. In most instances the core is the lowermost section of the butt rod-joint itself, but whether or no, the usual practise is to incorporate the handgrasp with its adjacent reel-seat inseparably with the butt-joint.

In contradistinction to this, the author wishes to emphasize at once his hearty agreement with the plan advocated by the late Henry P. Wells, of fitting to the rod an *independent grasp*, chiefly for its emi-nently practical value in preventing the rod from becoming permanently bent or set under unusually severe strain of casting or the playing of a heavy fish. With this arrangement the whole rod may be rotated at the handgrasp ferrule, so that it may be used either with the guides underneath or on its upper surface, the reel always remaining properly seated, on the under side of the reelseat; and the maximum strain thus is transferred alternately from one side of the rod to the other. A further innovation made by Mr. Wells (the law was his vocation though angling was his loved avocation) consisted in shaping the grasp more perfectly to the grip of the hand than had been the custom; and this whole device, combining the two distinctive features of separability and shape, has since been known to anglers as the " Wells grip."

It is true that a rod so built is increased in weight to the extent of the added pair of ferrules which are necessary for the seating of the butt-joint within the handgrasp — perhaps three-quarters of an ounce. But it is weight in a good place; furthermore, this may be offset by use of the extremely light yet very serviceable fly-rod reels that are available today, and by dispensing with the solid reelseat of metal in favor of simple *reel bands*, the so-called skeleton reelseat.

A metal reelseat is altogether unnecessary in the rod adapted for fly- and the lighter bait-fishing, and again, the inclusion of all this " tin " certainly adds nothing in elegance of finish to such a dainty contrivance. When it comes to the short, bait-casting rod, with the strenuous reel work that is imperative in its use and the manifest advantage here of some form of locking reel-band, that is an entirely different story, and we welcome the metal reelseat as a most appropriate feature of the rod, under these conditions.

Not only do we prefer the specially-shaped and independent grasp, but we like it very well when made of our common native red cedar — for the lightest rods and except for prolonged use. This makes a very attractive handle, as cedar is very light, is easily worked into shape, is of a pleasing color, takes a beautiful polish, and does not show soil after use.   It affords the best material for the reelseat, whether or no the grasp itself be made of cork.

The pattern of grasp that we shall illustrate fits the hand nicely and we shall therefore be at some pains to give the exact dimensions, and to explain just how it, with the reelseat, is built from one piece of wood.

You should, some months previously, have gone to the woods and chopped down a small cedar tree, which you have had ripped at the sawmill into boards 1½ inches thick, and which since then have been seasoning against the time when you would be ready to make use of them.   Your grasp you now proceed to carve out of a piece of this cedar, 1½ inches square and 10½ inches long; and it is not difficult, as already intimated.

The thing first to do is to bore a hole in the end that is to receive the female or socket ferrule, before any attempt is made at shaping the wood.   The ferrule size at the grasp, for a ten-foot rod, is ⁷⁄₁₆ inch, but the hole must receive the outside ferrule,

and *its outside* diameter is $^{15}\!/_{32}$ inch.   You will need
for this job a drill-bit, which you can obtain — with
a square shank for use in a brace — in this diameter; the wood-boring bits are more coarsely graded
in size than are drill-bits.   For the nine- or nine and
one-half-foot rod, the handgrasp ferrule is $^3\!/_8$ inch,
and you want a $^{13}\!/_{32}$-inch drill-bit for
boring for its handle socket.

Place the piece of cedar in the
vise at such an angle that will enable
you to sight conveniently along the
bit as you stand and bore; and bore
slowly, and as *straight* as possible
down the center of the wood, to the
required depth.

Now you want to find out just
how nearly you have succeeded in
centering that hole.   To do this,
take your butt-joint or any straight
stick that will serve — winding the
end with thread if necessary for a
snug fit — and thrust this down into
the cedar block to the full depth of
the boring.   Next sight along your
joint or stick and see if you have it

Fig. 1 — Independent
wood grasp

properly aligned with the grasp.
Most likely you will find that the
present condition of affairs is that represented in
Fig. 1 — you have quite a decided angular deflec-

tion between joint and grasp, despite all your care
to have that hole straight. In order to correct
this, by accurately centering the joint in its socket,
you must plane the cedar block down to one-inch
square, in the manner indicated by the dotted lines
of the illustration. You then sight along another
of the surfaces of the block, adjoining the surface
first marked as shown, and plane again as may
be necessary to straighten up the other two sides.
Now your hole *is* centered, and grasp will line with
rod, in all positions of rotation.

Withdraw the joint and you now are ready to
shape up your grasp. Cut a pattern of cardboard
or stiff paper to conform with the diagram, Fig. 2.

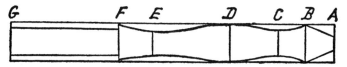

Fig. 2 — Wood grasp

The diameters are as follows, to which you can gauge
the finished grasp with a pair of calipers: At B,
one inch; C, $\frac{3}{4}$; D, $1\frac{1}{32}$; E, $1\frac{1}{16}$; F, $\frac{7}{8}$. Distances
are: A — G, $10\frac{1}{2}$ inches; A — B, 1 inch; B — C,
$\frac{3}{4}$; C — D, 2; D — E, $2\frac{1}{8}$; and F — G, $3\frac{5}{8}$. Lay
this pattern on two opposite faces of the cedar block
and trace the outline in pencil. Place the block in
the vise and cut away the wood with a chisel, from
A to F, down to the penciled lines. Then trace the

outline on the two remaining surfaces, and cut away
similarly. Next saw the part from F to G down to
a full ¾-inch square. You now have the whole
thing in the shape shown in Fig. 3.

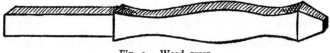

Fig. 3 — Wood grasp

Take your jack-knife and cut away the corners
equally, till the whole grasp is reduced from the
square to an octagonal shape on cross-section.

Next we seat the female ferrule. Before cementing this, get a winding-taper or -check (A, Fig. 4)
that fits nicely over the ferrule and up against the
welt; fit this over the thin edge of the wood, around
the mouth of the hole in the grasp, mortising it in
flush with the wood by filing a recess to receive it,
with the triangular saw-file, and cement it in position. This will guard against splitting of the grasp
as you force the ferrule into it; but for the first
attempt, it will be safer to seat the ferrule in the
cedar while in block form before starting to shape
the grasp. You now can melt some cement, spread
it evenly over the whole outside of the ferrule up
to the welt, as you hold it over the flame with a pair
of pliers, taking pains the while *not to get any on the
inside;* then thrust it into its hole, and by pushing
down hard against the floor or the solid door-jamb,

using your whole weight, *quickly* force it home to the welt.

Great care should be taken to have the hole positively accommodate the ferrule, though snugly, making use of a round (rat-tail) file to enlarge the boring if necessary to this end. The ferrule expands a bit on heating, and if the hole be too small the ferrule will stick before reaching the whole distance down into the grasp. Meanwhile the cement has cooled and thickened, and the only way that you now can remove the ferrule without injury is to split off the wood, making it necessary to *begin all over again.* Be encouraged however in your perseverance to have the grasp right, by the knowledge that when once completed one of these independent handles can be used for several different rods for the use of one angler — a nice insurance furthermore against the borrowing of your pet rods.

Finally, round up the whole with the convex surface of a wood-rasp or coarse file, followed by number 2 and then number 1 sandpaper; mount the reel-bands and fit the butt-cap. The sliding reel-band should have a milled raised edge to grip with the fingers. The German-silver butt-cap and reel-bands selected by the author are ¾ inch in diameter, and were obtained from the T. H. Chubb Rod Co., of Post Mills, Vermont, at a total cost of forty-six cents. Before cementing on the cap D, (Fig. 4), and in order to seat the reel securely, file a flat sur-

face on the side of the reelseat that corresponds with
the line-guides when grasp is jointed to the butt in
the position, with relation to rotation, that gives

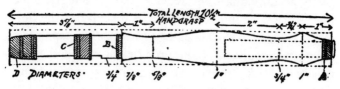

Fig. 4 — Wood grasp

the most perfect alignment of grasp and butt-joint.
It is a good plan to glue a little piece of leather
to this flat surface for the reel-plate to jam against
when the reel is seated; a strip of an old hat's sweat-
band is just the thing.

The completed grasp will appear as represented
in Fig. 4.   A indicates the taper hugging the ferrule-
welt, B is a band that largely is ornamental and may
be dispensed with, C is the reel-band proper, and D
is the butt-cap.

But when it comes to a real fighting implement,
and for continuous, prolonged usage, there is nothing in the same class with a solid-cork grasp for
the rod — not a mere veneer of cork; and to make
one of these you may proceed as we now will direct.

If you purpose making an independent grasp, first
you construct a short bamboo-section, not tapering
but of the same thickness throughout, and of the
proper size, when rounded, to receive snugly the

handgrasp ferrule, which is both cemented and *pinned* to one end of it, as shown in Fig. 5.

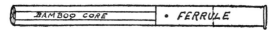

Fig. 5 — Independent cork grasp

Bore a short piece of cedar and shape its end to receive a metal taper, just as in making the all-cedar grasp; then slip this over the bamboo-core and up against the ferrule-rim (welt or shoulder) and cement it fast, as seen in Fig. 6. Next slip on and secure with glue or ferrule cement successive cork-ring sections sufficient for the needed

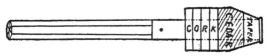

Fig. 6 — Cork grasp

length of the actual hand portion of the grasp. Cement them in place, several at a time, and allowing these to set before putting on the next installment. Jam the last ones you are placing, firmly against their predecessors by putting the bamboo-core between the vise jaws and pushing the cork up against the ends of the jaws; then tighten the vise and leave things awhile. It is a good idea to have the grain of each disk of cork to cross that of its neighbor.

These cork rings or solid disks that you can per-

forate as required, may be had of selected quality
from your tackle-dealer, or you can utilize the best
of large corks obtained from the paint or drug store,
such as are used for gallon cans or for the wide-
mouthed vaseline bottles.   To perforate these, you
file a cutting edge on the end of a brass ferrule or
other piece of metal tubing of suitable size; you
either may fit this with a handle, or secure it in the
vise by means of your wooden holder (see chapter

Fig. 7 — Cork grasp

on " Ferrules ") and bore the hole by turning the
cork backward and forward against its sharp end.

Finally, make a cedar reelseat of similar style to
that described above, but with a hole, an inch or
more in depth, bored into its front end for fitting
that over the other end of the bamboo-core and up
against the hindermost cork-ring, where it is glued
into place and reinforced by insertion of a piece of
the pointed end of a small brass escutcheon-pin.
Your cork-ringed fly-rod handgrasp now will be in
the state indicated by Fig. 7.   It remains to finish
up the reelseat, including the mounting of reel-bands
and butt-cap, as already detailed, and to work the
cork part or grasp proper down to shape as shown
by the dotted lines of the above illustration.   A file

cannot well be used here — it would tear the cork
— and the result is accomplished, after shaving to
approximate shape with a *sharp* thin knife- or razor-
blade, with sandpaper wrapped about a round stick
of about five-eighths inch in diameter.   This is manipulated with an oblique sliding and turning motion
— slide it away from you as you turn toward you.
Finish by twisting the grasp within a fold of fine
sandpaper held snugly in the left palm.

The process employed is somewhat different for

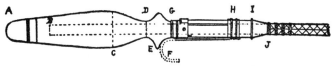

Fig. 8 — Cedar grasp for bait-casting rod

the bait-casting rod.   Here the grasp is not remov-
able, and because of the increased strain on the
handle of this rod, the butt-joint should extend down
inside the grasp to within two inches at most of
the butt-cap, this part of the joint first being filed
down to a uniform size.   In this rod the reelseat
is placed above the grasp.   A pattern for the handle
of cedar is shown in Fig. 8, one piece of wood extending from A to I.   G — I represents a German-silver
reelseat, slid over and cemented to its cedar-core.
This reelseat has a simple but effective locking reel-
band (H) and it was obtained from James Heddon's
Sons, of Dowagiac, Mich., for one dollar.   The

ridge at E projects between the first and second
fingers of the rod-hand, insuring a secure grip and
obviating the necessity for the somewhat ungainly
forefinger " trigger " (hook) with which many bait-
casting rods are equipped, as indicated by the dotted
lines at F. A is the butt-cap; B, the end of the

Fig. 9 — Cork grasp for bait-casting rod, with mushroom butt, and
finger-hook or trigger attached to reel-band

butt-joint. Measurements are: A — G, 5⅝ inches;
G — J, 4⅜ inches; C, 1⅛ inches; D, $^{21}/_{32}$ inch.

We rather favor a solid-cork grasp for this rod,
and like one with a cedar butt-cap of a mushroom
shape (Fig. 9). A shaped cork-grasp for a bait-
casting rod — and any other individual parts of
their standard models — may be purchased from
the Dowagiac people; and not only the individual
cork-rings or solid disks, already mentioned, but
cork-grip handgrasps, in a more or less finished state
and in a variety of patterns, are obtainable from
most of the larger tackle-houses.

ROD-MAKING:

VARNISHING AND FINISHING

CHAPTER X

ROD-MAKING: VARNISHING AND FINISHING

The prime requisites of a good rod-varnish are that it should possess a maximum degree of elasticity and form an efficient protecting coat against the penetration of moisture into the pores of the bamboo. A varnish that dries too hard chips easily and soon will crack under the repeated flexion of the rod. A "special" rod-varnish need not be sought, as the specifications are met in any of the best brands of *spar* varnish, put up by a number of the bigger varnish houses, such as Berry, Crockett, or Murphy. The author has more recently used Valentine's "Valspar."

Varnishing should be done in dry weather, preferably on a clear, snappy day, or on a warm day with little humidity. If this is not sufficiently explicit, have your wife or sweetheart pick out for you what she says is a good wash-day. And you should varnish indoor, in a warm room with air as free as possible from floating dust particles. A small camel's-hair or ox-hair brush, of the kind that we used for gluing (the same brush will do, if it was thoroughly cleaned), suits our present purpose likewise.

As already has been mentioned, the writer applies the first, diamond windings and the initial coat of varnish soon after the rod-joints are glued up and dry.   No attempt then is made to flow it on, but care is taken to have it worked thoroughly into and around all of the silk-windings, using short strokes of the brush in all directions. 'For this coat, the varnish may advantageously be thinned with turpentine — but *not adding more than twenty per-cent* — for better penetration of the silk; and likewise for the second application, which includes only the solid-wrappings about the guides and ferrule-ends, etc. When at this take care not to gum up the exposed metal parts.   Dilute the varnish but little, if at all, for the subsequent coats.   To insure a good flow, *have it warm while in use,* by standing its container in hot water.

A satisfactory way of keeping varnish for future use, after the original can has been opened, is to transfer it to a wide-mouthed bottle, which must be kept tightly corked; to be on the safe side against evaporation and thickening, cover the exposed part of the cork with melted paraffine.

Spar varnish being an elastic varnish, dries neither as hard nor as soon as does coach or cabinet varnish; some kinds of the latter may be rubbed within a few hours following a fresh application on a good drying day; but spar varnish should be given a day or two between coats before any attempt is made at rubbing-down. Varnished work will dry quickest out-of-door, in clear, dry weather and a brisk wind; but in order to escape the dust as much as possible, your rod-joints must be hung up inside for at least the first four or five hours, until dried dust proof; and hang them well away from the wall, else the varnish may " creep."

It is the practise of the author to apply five or six coats of varnish, in all, after the following manner: First, two thin applications, as explained above, given with circular or oblique strokes around the joint; two additional coats covering all, flowed on carefully and evenly by brushing in long, quick strokes lengthwise of the joint.   We then have the silk sufficiently protected to permit of rubbing the varnish down without injury to the windings.   This we now proceed to do, *lightly and cautiously this first time* and with increasing vigor after each of the succeeding two or three coats.

Some would object to so many coats of varnish on the ground of their being deleterious to the action of the rod. We think that such criticism is altogether theoretical, and that a much more practical point is that *moisture* penetrating the rod-wrappings and the pores of the bamboo is the great foe to the life of the rod and to the maintenance of its elasticity, and that a generous coating of the right kind of varnish furnishes the surest protection against this.

To rub down, use powdered rotten-stone — from drug or paint store — on a small square of canvas, or felt from an old soft hat, wet with cold water; this makes a fine brown mud with which you scrub the joints lengthwise between the thumb and fingers of one hand, while the other twirls the joint to and fro.   When the rubbing is completed, rinse the joint thoroughly with cold water squeezed out of a small fine sponge.   It is a good plan to let the water run with force, directly from the tap, on the parts about the guides.   Complete the cleaning by wiping with the sponge just damp.   Then wipe with a dry soft cloth and swish the joint a few times in the air completely to dry it.   Have it *perfectly dry before applying any more varnish,* and be sure that the rotten-stone is thoroughly cleaned with a bit of rag from under and around the guides.   Powdered pummice-stone and water may be used for rubbing the varnish coats that follow the first use of the rotten-stone; but at the first attempt at finishing a rod, perhaps you had best confine yourself to the rotten-stone.

In finishing the cedar handgrasp or any cedar parts, follow the filing and coarse sandpapering by using number 1 paper, then number 0, rotating the grasp forcibly between a fold of the paper held tightly in the palm of the left hand.   After a good

smooth surface is obtained, apply water with a
sponge, to raise the grain of the wood; when dry,
make a second application of fine sandpaper and
elbow-grease; give now two coats of varnish; rub
down with pummice-stone and water; apply a third
coat of varnish; rub with the wet rotten-stone or
with linseed oil and rotten-stone; give a fourth and
last coat of varnish, very lightly.

For the last finishing-touches both on joints and
handgrasp, rub with a bunch of curled horsehair
(see the upholsterer), then with a little " Three-in-
One " oil applied with a soft rag, then with a buck-
skin glove or piece of chamois-skin or felt, then with
an old silk-handkerchief; and in conclusion, apply
as much hand-friction with the heel of your palm
as your inclination and perseverance will allow.
The ultimate result is that you have produced on all
a smooth but not glassy finish, that is not dulled by
handling the rod — whose subdued luster is very
durable.   The whole rod now requires but an occasional rubbing with the silk-handkerchief and a few
drops of oil, and the application of a single light
coat of varnish about every second season if used
regularly.

At last, my Brother of the Angle, your rods are
completed in every fascinating detail — and if they
do not appear as the illustrations depict, and are not
a delight to your eye and a joy to your hand, it is

not because the writer has failed to tell you, so far as mind can recall, every blamed thing that he knows about this business. Suspend them from the tip, safe from the kiddies' curious investigations, feast your eyes soulfully upon their charms, and, upon occasion, you even may take them down and fondle them lovingly; then, when the first feathered harbingers of the coming Spring begin their blithesome twitterings — and not till then — haste you now to rig them up and experience that exquisite thrill of their feel in action, as you test them out on the nearest piece of greensward, if a suitable stretch of water be not conveniently accessible. And you now may say, " as one having authority," if you think that an honestly hand made Split-Bamboo is worth its price; and if you agree with me that the building thereof is a poem, the perusing of which is a thing well calculated to assist in passing profitably many an hour in delightfully novel and restful diversion, oblivious to carking cares.

SPLIT-BAMBOOS OF THE AUTHOR'S MAKE

1—Eight-foot fly-rod, 4½ ounces, integral cork grasp
2—Nine-foot fly-rod, 5½ ounces, detachable cork grasp
3—Nine-and-one-half-foot fly-rod, 6 ounces (same grasp)
4—Ten-foot fly-rod, 6¾ ounces, detachable cork grasp
5—Five-and-one-quarter-foot bait-casting rod, cedar grasp, and with light and heavy tops

CULTIVATING SILKWORM-GUT
AT HOME

By Edwin T. Whiffen

(By kind permission of the author
and of *Forest and Stream*)

CHAPTER XI

CULTIVATING SILKWORM-GUT AT HOME

By Edwin T. Whiffen

After a little experience every angler with the fly who is in the habit of studying the problems that constantly confront him recognizes the importance of concealing the connection between the line and the lure. Such a connection is established by means of the leader, consisting usually of silkworm-gut imported from Spain. Now the desirable qualities in a leader are strength, fineness, and unobtrusiveness. This last essential depends upon color, absence of luster, and of any small peculiarities which serve to call attention to any particular part of the leader. In its ordinary state, the Spanish gut offends against all three just-mentioned qualities; its color is obtrusive, it possesses a shine that makes it a target for every eye, and the frequent knots mean just so many points to distract the fish's attention from the object of the angler's special interest — the artificial fly. The shine may be removed by one of the processes known as " drawing," that is, taking off the outer layer of the gut by means of sandpaper; but this unduly weakens the product. The leader may be artificially colored, and this also is usually a weakening process. The knots, like the poor, we have with us always.

As a result of the study of these conditions, I became convinced years ago that a substitute for the Spanish-gut leader was a matter of desire for the angler.

As the Spanish " gut " is the product of the silk-sacs of the Asiatic silkworm, the idea naturally presented itself of endeavoring to substitute a larger caterpillar, and one with larger silk-sacs, for the insect from which the Spanish gut is derived. This substitute was sought for in the various American bombycid (family *bombycidæ*) or silkworm larvæ. Of all our American varieties, the caterpillar spinning the largest cocoon is that of the cecropia moth (*Platysamia cecropia*). The general color of this moth is a rusty red or brown; this is the color of the head and foreparts. It has a distinctive white collar; the abdomen is reddish, and has bands of black and white; the wings are grayish with bands of red and white extending across them. A characteristic is the transparent membrane or eye-spot which is found on the fore wing; a whitish crescent or kidney-shaped spot marks the rear wings; and the whole wing has a clayish-brown edge. The antennæ or " horns " are broad and feathery, those of the male being much more so than those of the female and thus furnishing an easy means of distinguishing the sexes.

The full-grown cecropia caterpillar averages from three to four inches in length but when very large may measure nearly five inches, is moderately stout,

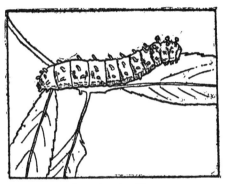

Cecropia caterpillar

and of an apple-green color.   On the various seg-ments of the body are tubercles or shot-like append-ages mounted on the ends of little stalks.   On the second, third, and fourth segments these tubercles are of a coral color; on other segments they may be blue or black.   The head is green with black mark-ings.   These features characterize the full-grown worm.

Next in size as a spinner of cocoons is the *Tele-polyphemus*.   The polyphemus moths are nearly as large as those of cecropia, and they vary in color somewhat more than the latter moth.   The general impression is a reddish or yellow, furry brown, with black scales peppering the wings, on which are cross-bands of red or pink, white, and gray.   On each wing is the typical eye-spot, and a transparency sur-

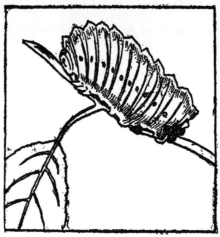

Polyphemus caterpillar

rounded first by a lightish brown circle, and by a black ring outside of this.   Like the cecropia, the sexes are distinguished by the difference in breadth of the antennæ.   The color of the bodies is a dark or light tan, and the forepart has a gray band.   The cocoon is ovoid in shape, when first spun looking as if dusted over with lime; later the color is brown. The caterpillar spins on practically the same kinds of bushes or trees as the cecropia.   In the spinning process, the worm does not break the thread to form a means of egress at the front of the cocoon, as the cecropia does; hence the long thread may be reeled off, and might furnish a valuable fiber. The film when thus unwound from the cocoon has a beautiful silver tint, and is surprisingly strong for its size.

The caterpillar reaches an extreme length of three inches or little more, and it is plumper for its length than the cecropia. The general color is blue-green on the back and yellow-green on the sides. Yellow tubercles are found on the back and sides, arranged in lines.

A caterpillar much resembling polyphemus is luna (*Actias luna*). The line on the anal plate is yellow, instead of brown, and the worm is of a different shade of green; and thus may be readily distinguished. It spins a thinner cocoon, and probably has little value as a gut-producer.

Among the smallest of this class of the moths is the *Callosamia promethea*, whose method of attaching its cocoon distinguishes this phase of its existence from the preceding varieties. A handle, like an umbrella's, securely holds the cocoon to the twig or leaf-stem. This is a pretty little moth, but the results of my experiments with it go to show that as a producer of gut it is a failure, the strand being small, short, and weak.

An imported variety, from China, is the cynthia or ailanthus silkworm. Its cocoon and method of attachment resembles those of promethea. It produces a slightly longer and larger length of gut.

As a fact, none of the American silkworms are worth bothering with as gut-producers in comparison with cecropia; although I have secured fairly good, stout strands of gut, four or five feet long, from polyphemus. But my experience has been that a small cecropia caterpillar produces as much gut, and of a better quality, than a large polyphemus; while a big cecropia is unapproachable in this respect, yielding a strand of gut from six to nine feet long, round, smooth, of a suitable color, lusterless, and *knotless*. Polyphemus is not worth raising if cecropia can be obtained.

By hunting, available material for the cultivation of these worms may be obtained in the shape of moths, cocoons, eggs, and caterpillars, the cocoon state being on the whole the most satisfactory. In length, the cecropia cocoons vary from somewhat over an inch (very small) to three inches (very large). Some are slender and compactly spun, others are loosely spun and baggy. They vary in color, when fresh, being brownish, and when weathered, somewhat silvery. They are more pointed at one end than at the other. Careful examination of this pointed end shows that the threads were broken and then puckered together in the process of spinning. The cocoon usually is attached to the side of the twig, branch, tree-trunk, or stalk on which

Polyphemus moth
—one-quarter
life size

Promethea—
half-grown worm,
adult, and
new cocoon,
on one bush

the caterpillar has chosen to spin. The caterpillar
may elect to spin on its food-plant, or it may wander
away and spin on almost any suitable stalk or twig.
Its cocoon has been found on maple, willow, wood-
bine, oak, plum, elder, wild cherry, spicewood, apple,
pear, nettle, wild hemlock, sumach, ailanthus, and
other varieties " too numerous to mention."

It is worth while to look almost anywhere in a
locality in which cocoons are being found.   Usually
there is more or less of a little colony discoverable
where a single cocoon has been discovered. You
may pick a cocoon plastered to the trunk of a tree
at its very root, or attached to a shoot but a few
inches from the ground; then as you glance up you
notice the brown, baggy bunch thirty feet in the air,
spun alongside the tip of the twig.   No place is too
unusual or insignificant to be overlooked, though one
soon develops a special sense in searching.

Your equipment for cocoon-hunting need not be
elaborate.   There are some things that are helpful,
if not really necessary.   You can put in your pocket
the cocoons that you find, if you wish, though there
is danger of crushing them; a bag or a box of some
kind is better.   If you are abroad in the Spring,
when the moth is laying its eggs, some little paper or
tin boxes will make good receptacles for your
" finds."   In the same season you will need larger
boxes in which to put any moths you may capture,
and a net will be necessary for taking the specimens.

In Summer or early Fall, the caterpillar season, some boxes large enough to hold your captures without crushing them will be advisable.   As for clothing, wear the oldest and toughest you have.   It is not especially conducive to the beauty of head-, foot-, or body-gear to go crushing through bushes, briars, and shrubs, over bogs and swamps, or to crowd up trees and into other places difficult of access in which some caterpillars seem to have taken a fiendish delight to spin.   An umbrella with a crook for a handle is helpful in pulling down branches or twigs just out of one's unaided reach, where frequently fat cocoons are attached.   A fish-line with a weight on the end is serviceable for bringing down those branches a little too high for the umbrella.   If you are working among trees of any size, a long pole with a triangle-hook attached will enable you to reach cocoons spun by worms of the most aspiring spirit. The most valuable item in your equipment you will not be able to take with you at first — a general ability to distinguish good territory from bad and to " smell out " every specimen in the locality.

Let us suppose it is Fall or early Winter, and you are hunting cecropia and polyphemus.   You should follow along the road or street studying carefully the trees and shrubbery. Luckily enough for the hunter, cocoons as a rule are not found in high, dense vegetation or inside of groves or woods.   Circle around the outside of such places, studying carefully

every tree and shrub, low or high. Examine any
tuft of leaves or protuberance on twig or trunk.
Pass over nothing that at all suggests what you are
in search of. Sometimes it is a good plan to study
a clump of bushes or a tree from one direction and
then slowly circle it so that the light will be thrown
on the leaves and limbs from various angles.

If you are in the street, you may collect a small
crowd anxious to see "what the gink is rubberin'
at," but a true explorer never pays any attention to
little things like that. A vacant city lot which has
many or few bushes, stumps with sprouts springing
from them, little, weazened trees that almost apolo-
gize for living, sometimes yield surprising finds. A
lane in the suburbs with trees and bushes on either
side furnishes good hunting-ground. If there is a
wall on either side with a vine of some sort growing upon it, you may find that careful search will
reveal brown, baggy bunches that prove to be cecropia cocoons. Patches of scrub white-birch or spice-
bush should always be carefully examined, as such
places often harbor many cocoons.

Cocoons may be hunted for at any time after the
spinning season until the warm Springtime weather
causes the moths to emerge from the cocoons. As
soon as possible after the falling of the leaf is the
best time, as certain birds tear apart the cocoons
and eat the tender pupæ within. Places in the cities
and suburban towns are usually more productive of

results to the cocoon-hunter, not necessarily because there are more cocoons, but because the cocoons are more in view and closer together on account of there being fewer trees and shrubs to attract the female moth as it lays its eggs. Almost the best place of all is a field with numerous scattered clumps of willow, maple, spice-bush, or alder; these usually are small and accessible. The adult moth, on its egg-laying mission, seems to find dense vegetation a hindrance and hence avoids it.

The caterpillars probably do not stay many feet from the spot where they hatched from the egg; indeed, the worm may pass all stages of its life-history and spin its cocoon on a single shrub. Sometimes such unpromising spots as backyards are well worthy of search. The egg-laying function of the moth is compulsive and the eggs must be laid wherever the parent may chance to be at the proper time of depositing them. It has from two hundred to six or eight hundred eggs to dispose of in a comparatively short time, and cannot afford to be too nice as to the character of the place where it deposits them.

The American silkworm caterpillars have various parasitical enemies, particularly varieties of the ichneumon-flies. The adult parasite lays its eggs on the body of the caterpillar; there hatch out and the tiny worms proceed to eat their way into the body of their host, which soon may die. Or the cater-

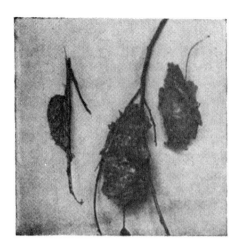

Cecropia
cocoons of
different size
and shape

Cecropia
cocoon
showing
the details

pillar may live long enough to perform its functions of spinning but then dries up and dies. Or the parasite may construct a peculiar kind of cocoon within the larger one spun by the host; such specimens are interesting to the scientist but valueless to the one who wishes to rear caterpillars from the egg. As a rule, specimens which have not pupated are easily distinguishable from good ones. The silk of such cocoons is thinner, and when the cocoon is shaken close to the ear a peculiar dry rattle is heard; a good specimen when similarly treated gives a characteristic, unmistakably solid *thud*. Those specimens in which parasites have pupated are not thus distinguishable; only by opening the cocoon and examining the contents can the counterfeit be detected. It is not well to disturb the pupa in this way; it is better to watch carefully for the emergence of the wasp-like ichneumonides, which should be destroyed when they are perceived.

While the idea of collecting the cocoons and of getting a supply of eggs from the moths is unmistakably the best plan, do not be in despair if your cocoon-hunt is unsuccessful. You may be able to capture one or more fertile females in the Spring, which will supply you eggs from which enough caterpillars will hatch to keep you sufficiently busy. For this variety of " bug-hunting " you will need a net of some light mosquito-mesh, with tin or paper boxes in which to stow away your captures.

The American silkworm moths generally fly by night, and the electric light is hence a blessed institution to the moth-hunter. These creatures, some of them as large as a small bat, or, perhaps a better comparison, as broad as your hand, and of the most entrancing beauty in shape, color, and silken flight, will throw even the beginner into raptures at their sight. Some alight gracefully and stand slowly furling and unfurling their wings, as if pardonably proud of their beauty. Some float like a many-hued shadow to and fro. In either case a skillful turn of the net effects a capture. A morning search is sometimes profitable. The moths are occasionally found hanging to the roofs or beams of sheds; the undersides of bridges, if near lights, are likely places. Sometimes you will see the moths bobbing against the window-screen from the outside, where they may be taken. The cecropia, especially the female, throws off a peculiar "animal odor," by which it may be tracked to its hiding-place in the daytime. This odor is exceedingly strong, almost offensively so, and is carried by the wind to a considerable distance; it aids the male to find the female, at the mating season. Once smelled you will never forget it.

At this time of the year, egg-hunting may yield fair results. Suitable places evidently are about the same as for the cocoons. You should carry along tin boxes with covers, in which to place the leaves upon which the eggs are found; remove the leaf entire, to avoid injuring the eggs in any way; examine both sides of all the leaves of shrubs in a promising locality.

Cecropia eggs are of an ovoid shape. On the upper side is a reddish spot, and they are about as large as quite small bird shot. The polyphemus lays white, brown-banded eggs which are larger than those of cecropia. Both species deposit eggs in a variety of ways, sometimes singly, sometimes in a short row, or in peculiar little masses.

Last, and least satisfactory of all, is the method of attempting to find the caterpillars. They hide away so cunningly as to be nearly undiscoverable, even when the signs of their presence are unmistakable. Such signs are wholly- or partly-eaten leaves and the presence of excrement on the ground beneath. Just previous to the actual spinning, the worm may crawl along in an excited fashion, as though anxious to reach a certain spot on schedule time; it may then be found almost anywhere, running up or down a tree trunk, or along the road, or across a walk. Such specimens do not ordinarily give a satisfactory strand of gut, as the chances are against their having eaten of the kind of leaf that results in the best variety of that product.

In case you have secured a reasonable number of cocoons, twenty or so, it is best to put them away in a cold place during the Winter. A good plan is to place them in a small screen-cage and expose them

to the weather outside; the moisture and the cold of
Winter will not work any injury but will keep the
cocoons and their contents from becoming too dry.
If they are not thus exposed, it is well to turn them
occasionally and sprinkle them lightly with water.

When the weather becomes warm in Springtime
and the leaf-buds begin to appear, bring your cocoons
into a warm room, when the moths soon will begin
to emerge.   If so situated as to be able to have a
-oom for rearing purposes, the moths may be allowed
to fly around free from confinement.   If a male and
a female of the same species emerge at about the
same time, they usually will mate without any difficulty.   After the completion of this function the
male soon dies, and the female immediately begins
to deposit eggs.   It lays several hundred in the
course of a few nights, and then dies too, neither
sex living more than a week or ten days.   In case
a female or females alone should emerge from the
cocoon stage, a mate must be secured if the eggs are
to be fertile.   This is done by exposing the female
out of doors, either in a screen-box with large inter-
stices or else by securing her by tying a length of
woolen yarn about her "waist," the other end of
this tether being made fast to prevent her escape.
The former method is preferable, as bats and birds
are fond of a tender moth.   If you place the captive
moth outside the window, be sure that it is on the
side of the house opposite to the direction in which

the wind is blowing, so that the scent may be carried farthest and be most likely to attract a mate. If your attempt is successful, the evidence usually will be found in the presence of the male in the morning.

The fertile female moth should be placed in a pasteboard box with a cover, such as a shoe box, where it will " get busy " and plaster every available place with eggs, at the same time battering its beautiful wings pitifully. As soon as all the eggs of a moth have been deposited, on the sides, bottom, and cover of the box, with a sharp knife remove them on a little bit of the paper, being very careful not to crack the hard, shiny shells, as they will thus be spoiled. Put the eggs, thus removed, into *tight* tin-boxes or glass jars (Mason jars), and put the covers on tightly unless you wish to find wandering baby caterpillars, looking for " something good," scattering over the neighborhood. At all times, but especially when they are small, should tight receptacles for your worms be supplied, as they will go through a pin-hole, with several feet to spare in every direction, for they are great roamers.

The hatching period may be as short as seven days, but usually is ten days, or even more if the weather is cool. Shortly before hatching, the eggs become quite dark in color; then the little " darkies " eat a hole and crawl out, soon looking too large ever to have been able to get into so small a compass.

Their appearance should have been carefully watched for, and food leaves have been supplied as soon as the little, black worms were seen. The freshly-hatched cecropia caterpillar is about a quarter of an inch long, black, and with little black bristle-like tubercles. Occasionally I have had freaks in a brood, such specimens being a deep yellow in color. Any kind of leaf which the young caterpillar will take is suitable food for the first three stages of its existence; one year, when I had a brood hatch early in April, I fed them on the leaf of some perennial shrub which supplied the only " garden sass " then available. I have seen it stated that the young Asiatic silkworm may be fed on lettuce for a few days, till better food may be obtained, but my experience with the young American silkworm is just the contrary; broods coming out before the leaves opened have " turned up their noses " at tender lettuce and stolidly succumbed to starvation.

Apple, pear, currant, peach, plum, berry of all kinds, bay, hard and soft maple, mountain laurel, apricot, may be fed to them, some broods preferring one kind, some another. They eat voraciously, with a peculiar movement; supporting themselves by the false legs or props on the latter half of the body, and grasping the edge of the leaf with the sharp-pointed true legs, they raise the head and set the mandibles into the edge of the leaf, then bring the head slowly down, at the same time cutting the leaf away with their rapidly-moving jaws — somewhat as the barber's instrument " dehaired " our locks just before the summer vacation, " to keep the boys cool." After a full meal the caterpillar rests awhile, digests its dinner, and then goes at it again. No wonder they grow like pigs!

In a few days the caterpillar's size has so increased that its skin is too small and must be exchanged for a larger one; in fact, the larger one already is developing. The caterpillar then " moults "; it refuses all food and ceases to move about, remaining still as if dead. If lightly touched, it jerks from side to side to testify its displeasure at being disturbed. It should be treated with great care as it is very easily injured at this time. Do not touch it with the hands at all if you can possibly help it; lift it, if necessary, by the leaf or twig to which it clings. Indeed, at all times handle your worm like Izaak Walton's frog, " as though you loved him; " the tender skin is easily torn, then infection may set in and death follow.

After a period of two or three days thus spent, the caterpillar is ready to moult. The mask-like headpiece may be seen hanging down in front of the face; and the colors of the caterpillar are dingy and dirty. Then the worm begins to wriggle; the old skin splits near the head, and the caterpillar, bright and fresh as though newly enameled, crawls out — like an emblem of the resurrection. Sometimes the

" mask " attached to the head is not shed with the rest of the skin and must be carefully removed. After the first moult the caterpillar regains its original color.

At all times be careful to have the receptacles for your worms scrupulously clean; every day remove the wilted leaves and dead caterpillars and thoroughly clean their quarters with a stiff brush, taking out every particle of dirt. Do not pull the caterpillars from the old leaf; put the fresh leaves into the cage and the worms will leave the old for the new, and the old ones may then be removed. A few fine drops of water should be sprinkled on the leaves every day, which the caterpillars search out and slowly drink them; but do not put in enough water to saturate the air in the receptacle. As for the receptacles or cages themselves, small tin-boxes will do well enough at first, but glass jars are better as their rounding bottoms are more easily kept clean. Give your specimens plenty of room, putting only a few into one cage unless it is very large. While the caterpillar has no objection to eating in the dark and under any circumstances can " get its hand to its mouth," I prefer a transparent cage, as then I can more readily keep track of the progress of the inmates. These cages may be nearly air-tight as worms respire very little.

Dry, roomy quarters are essential to prevent the development and spread of certain fungoid diseases.

If conditions are not right the caterpillar loses its appetite; its plump, firm appearance is changed to a thin and watery one; its skin cracks, and a whitish mold appears which soon kills the diseased worm. Dead or sickly specimens should be removed at once; and the cage should be thoroughly scalded and dried to kill any remaining germs. A little precaution, taken every day, will prevent such disastrous happenings and assure the successful maturing of the brood.

While I have been writing, the caterpillars have been feeding and growing; in a week or so they have developed sufficiently to be ready for the second moult. The process of resting, cessation from feeding, and shedding of skin is repeated; after this moult the color is distinctively yellow, and the larger tubercles are apparent. The worms should now be thinned out, some in each cage being transferred to another. Always be sure that the new receptacle is clean. Remember, the conditions of success are two: perfect cleanliness, and sufficient food of a proper kind; under these conditions the caterpillars thrive like young chicks. After a somewhat longer period of feeding — and they will keep you busy gathering leaves — they moult for the third time. At this stage their heads are green with black markings; the bodies have become yellow and have two rows of black dots running from " stem to stern ". The large black, red, and yellow tubercles might cause them to be thought in the final stage; but they now crave more food than before and fairly cram themselves with the leaves supplied to them.   At this stage you should begin feeding the *leaf suited to insure the very best quality of gut.*   I have found this to be, first, fleshy, juicy leaves from the plum tree, and a close second, the prickly leaves of the long blackberry, which the caterpillars munch down with much gusto.   You ought to have left, in spite of accident, disease, and death, at least half or two-thirds of your hatching, or some two hundred or so healthy and flourishing crawlers.   Listen as they eat, after you have put in fresh leaves for them in the morning; the sound will remind you of a gentle fall of rain in Summer.

If they ate before, they cram, gorge, distend, stuff themselves now.   In a week or ten days they should be ready for the final moult, from which they emerge hungrier than ever.   Their color is much as before, but the size of the head seems enormous.   In a week or ten days more they have grown to be four or five inches long and are very plump and sleek; then they cease feeding and prepare for the important process of spinning.   First they empty the digestive system entirely, excreting a thick, syrupy fluid.   Up to this time the excrement had been fairly firm, and this marked change in its consistency is an indication that spinning may be expected soon.

During the last stage it is a good plan to put the

worms out of doors to feed, selecting the most suit-
bale food-plant for them, as I have thought that the
gut produced by this treatment was of superior quality. Whether that idea is fancy or fact may be de-
batable; but this I do know, that it is much easier
for the one who has the job of looking after it to
bring the worm to its fodder than to bring its fodder
to the worm. They may grow somewhat larger in
this way, as there is never any lack of food; and
especially at this stage they eat so fast that they need
feeding two or three times a day, instead of only
once as during the previous moults. Now, and especially when I had large numbers, I have sometimes
used small branches with their leaves placed in Mason jars containing water; although I found a tendency on the part of the caterpillars to crawl down
after a drink and so drown themselves. My usual
method of feeding has been to put the loose leaves
(cut or torn on the edges when the caterpiller is
small) right into the cage, and to change food at
least once a day. Some labor can be saved by using
this plan of putting the twigs with leaves into bottles
or jars containing water; but to prevent the untimely
loss of some of your " star boarders," wind wool
or tie cotton around the twig just above where it
enters the neck of the bottle or jar, so that all sui-
cidal actions may be frustrated. Once I matured a
brood of cecropias by means of the " branch-and-
bottle " method, on the top of a square piano; the

jars tipped over sometimes and the water ran down into the " inwards " of the instrument, but it was only the piano that suffered — the worms thrived.

When, then, you find the soft, fluid excrement in the cage you may know that one or more of the caterpillars soon will begin to spin. The worm shortens somewhat, as the body-cavity contains little except the empty digestive system and the sacs with the fluid silk. These are two, long, transparent tube-like organs, each about eighteen inches long, of about the diameter of a steel knitting-needle, and curiously coiled and involved in the cavity of the

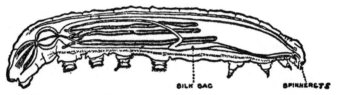

SILK SAC   SPINNERETS

Section of Asiatic silkworm (enlarged) showing silk-sac and spinnerets

body. At their front ends they connect with small tubes or spinnerets through which the caterpillar forces the fluid silk in shaping the material with which it spins. The spinning process is a most interesting one. When it is imminent the caterpillar crawls restlessly around, seeking a suitable place, and a short film of silk may be seen hanging down from its mouth. If you want to keep some cocoons over Winter for the next season, put the prospective spinner by himself into a glass receptacle with a few leaves, and watch proceedings.

After satisfying itself that it has selected a suitable place, the caterpillar firmly grasps a twig with the false legs or props, and with the true legs on the forward part of the body pulls the ends or sides of leaves together. Then the head moves up and down, back and forth, a film of sticky silk meanwhile gripping the leaves and holding them together. The worm works industriously, and soon the general outline and size of the cocoon appear, half-hidden in the leaves. In a few hours the caterpillar has spun sufficiently to hide itself from sight. If you wait a week or so and then carefully open the end of the cocoon, you will see an interesting sight; in place of the caterpillar, which was the last living thing observed in the cocoon at the beginning of the spinning process, a brownish pupa is seen, being a sort of case containing the embryonic organs of the future moth. Most of the cocoon, inside of the closely-woven exterior, will be a mass of fluffy silk-filaments surrounding a hard inner case, apparently lined with some compact, gum-like substance and containing besides the pupa the cast-off skin, now shriveled, brown, and crowded out of the way into the back of the cocoon.

Of course you will want to draw the gut from most of the worms which you have raised. The first important matter is to know the right time for the operation. After a little experience you will be able to tell by the film hanging from the caterpillar's mouth that the worm is what is technically known as " ripe; " but until that proficiency is developed you will more safely wait until the spinning has actually begun. Then prepare the solution in which to pickle the ripe worms. The proportions are: a sufficient quantity of vinegar (depending upon the number of worms ready) into which put enough salt to make a saturate solution, diluted with the same quantity of water. The salt should be put in the vinegar and thoroughly stirred until all the salt possible has been dissolved. Pour off the vinegar, leaving the undissolved salt, and then add the equal quantity of water. I have thought that vinegar in which the " mother " had formed was best for the purpose. You need not prepare more than a cupful ordinarily, as the caterpillars will ripen only a few at a time; and many of them may be pickled in one solution before it is used up. The purpose of the pickling process is to toughen the silk-sacs sufficiently to permit of their being pulled out. Into the solution, prepared as above, put whatever worms may be ready to spin, first tearing them across the back at about a quarter or a third of the distance from the head; but do not entirely remove or separate the torn portion of the worm.

While the pickling process is proceeding let me say that some have drawn gut without putting the worm into a solution of any kind.   I have tried this method on cecropia and polyphemus, but with unsatisfactory results.   I am not denying the possibility of doing it; I merely am stating my own experience.   I try a few worms by this method from every brood that I raise, and hope some day to be successful.   My experience has been that the unpickled sacs are too weak to permit of being drawn out in this way; however, I will describe this method in hopes that it may be useful to others.   Take a board from six to nine feet long.   Pin the worm securely to one end, putting one pin through the " tail " of the animal and two more about a third of the way back from the head.   With a sharp knife cut off the anterior part back nearly to the two pins. Take a large pin and dip it into the silk and carefully draw out as far as the fluid silk will go, and fasten each strand with a pin; a cecropia caterpillar has two silk-sacs and yields two strands of gut.   Let the gut thus drawn out dry in the shade for several days. I have read that a method like this has been successfully tried in France; but I must confess that I do not enjoy the experience — neither does the worm.   Very likely the caterpillar could be killed or stupefied by some means before the pinning was done.

The method which I employ has at least the merit of being more merciful.   After the worm has pickled for about half an hour I examine and draw out one end of a sac; and if it is strong and firm I continue the drawing process. If there is a suggestion of weakness I continue the pickling process fifteen or twenty minutes longer. I am convinced by experience that the precise moment for pulling out the sacs is a highly important consideration. If the pickling has been too short, the gut, while apparently strong and of good quality, seems to be lacking in the proper consistency; on the other hand, if the pickling is carried too far, the resulting strand is lumpy, and the lumpy parts while looking strong are really the weakest.

I do not feel that I can describe the exact point for drawing at which results are likely to be the best, though I could easily show to another the silk-sac when it had the proper consistency to assure them. But I will attempt a description, as even a poor one may be of some help though experience and observation are the best instructors. At its best condition for securing results, the sac on being removed from the body of the worm has a peculiar whitish appearance, not soft or mushy and yet not hard like a string of glue. The strand when pulled out suggests in appearance a tendon or " cord," such as is found in meat before cooking it — it has a peculiar, " glairy " look. This color becomes somewhat opalescent on drying and later may turn even dark brown.

Having satisfied yourself that the sac is properly pickled, work quickly, since there are, as stated, two strands to every worm and the pickling process must not unduly be prolonged. On the shady side of the veranda or of the house stick a pin into the clap-boards and tie to it securely one end of the sac. Then take the other end of the sac in the fingers or tie it to another pin and draw the gut out to its full length. If any parts of the sac are not fully drawn out these will be lumpy and weak when the gut is dry. Fasten the end of the sac just drawn out and allow it to dry for several days. While the gut must be stretched far enough to keep it from being lumpy, a little allowance must be made for contraction in the drying process; so ease up an inch or two before both ends of the gut are made fast. I have had very good success when the gut was drawn on a rainy day and the strands became moist and slack; in such circumstances I have thought that the gut was peculiarly strong. But at all events keep it out of the sun, and if it contracts so much as to pull out the pin at either end, refasten with the tension eased up somewhat. In a day or two you usually will find that you have a variety of colors; some will turn a dark golden-brown, some may have a bluish tint, others will be light like a washed-out rootlet or fiber, and still others will approximate in shade the ordinary Spanish gut but will lack the " shine " which the latter unfortunately possesses.

Restrain the tendency to use the freshly-drawn gut too soon; although it may be fine in texture and apparently strong, it should thoroughly mature for several days or even weeks, for best service. Once properly prepared, it will give good use for years. I have in my possession two leaders drawn ten years ago, yet they still are reliable.

I had to learn by experience that a careful maturing of the product is essential to success. On one occasion I had drawn several hundred leaders, but they were placed in a tin box before they were dry and were stored in a damp place; on examining them several weeks later I found about twenty of them still good, but the rest had become ruined from mildew.

Do not expect that every leader you draw out will be a good one. The Spanish gut sold in this country is but a small part of the total product, and not one strand in a hundred is perfect. So, much of your product will come out flat and weak, like the inferior strands of Spanish gut, due perhaps to improper pickling, the wrong kind of feed for the caterpillar, or to an unhealthy worm. A considerable number will be of fair strength, testing to three or four pounds, and sufficiently strong for brook-trout fishing; and occasionally you will get a fine specimen, long, round, and strong enough to hold a bass on fly tackle.

Naturally the strands will require testing to select the good from the bad. Tie a loop in one end of the strand and attach it to a hook or nail in the

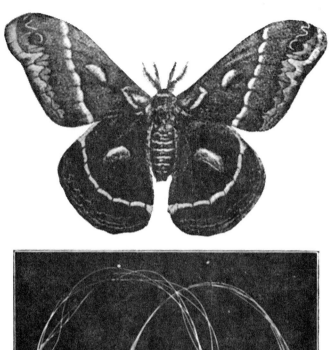

Cecropia moth, which in life may have a five-inch wing spread

Two of Mr. Whiffen's one-strand, home-grown Cecropia leaders, six feet long

wall.   Give it a moderately strong pull, holding by
the other end.   If the strand breaks easily or near
the middle, it usually is wise to discard it, although
it may be fine in texture and apparently strong; yet
I have had strands break near the middle in this
way, which on being fastened together by loops
made successful leaders.   The thin end usually is
the weakest part and may break off a few inches at
a time till two feet or more have been removed.
Now take those that stand this preliminary test
successfully and give them a more severe one.   Take
a milk bottle, for example, and put enough water in
it to make it weigh say three pounds; then attach
the strands to be tested and see if they will raise,
one at a time, that weight.   If they do they are
strong enough for trout-fishing with light tackle.
If you desire to select any leaders for bass fishing,
some which will show a greater strength, study very
carefully the leaders you have just tested and take
the largest, strongest-looking strands and with your
milk bottle filled to five- or six-pounds' weight, test
them again.   A fair proportion of the gut drawn
from a brood of cecropia worms should stand this
latter test.

With regard to those leaders that have "come
through," you will have a product from six to nine
feet long, of a slight taper, uniform in consistency,
even in color and strength, and which in appearance
will surpass the Spanish fine drawn-gut.

In one respect the inferiority of the American product must be admitted; I have not yet succeeded in producing a strand of gut that will test to ten or twelve pounds, as I understand an occasional strand of Spanish gut has done. Still, the extreme length of the imported article is eighteen to twenty inches, while the native product is three or four times as long. Strands tied together are not as strong as the single one, because the knot is the weakest part of the leader; therefore a leader testing up to eight or nine pounds is a very strong one. It is not improbable that a better variety of food, or a different pickling solution, or a careful breeding of worms to secure desired qualities, may produce an article superior to anything which I have been able to get, thus far. I have gone about the matter in an amateurish way and have produced results far exceeding my first hopes.

I consider the field a promising one. A first-class salmon-leader, for instance, is listed at five dollars, and is the product of several Asiatic silkworms. A cecropia strand of equal length and testing up to four or five pounds has been produced. As already noted, a cecropia caterpillar has two silk-sacs and yields two strands of gut. It is possible, therefore, that with really scientific study and manipulation one cecropia worm might produce ten-dollars' worth of gut. If one caterpillar in a hundred did, the occupation of raising them would be profitable. The raw materials — cocoons, moths, eggs, or caterpillars — cost nothing to collect, and at present very little to buy. Surely some person of more scientific bent than myself, with persistence and research, will work out a product which will be the best of its kind.

LANDING-NETS AND OTHER EQUIPMENT

CHAPTER XII

LANDING-NETS AND OTHER
EQUIPMENT

In Oppian's *Halieutica,* a poem of the second century A. D., the outfit of the perfect angler is summed up in the following couplet:

> The slender woven net, the osier creel,
> The tapering reed, the line; and barbèd steel.

Brethren, I would invite your attention for a few minutes to the consideration of that net.

Ever had it catch in the brush, stretch its rubber loop to the limit, then let go and, zip! soak you one in the back? or dangle, whether at the front or side, where you continually are getting tangled up in it, or where your flies become caught therein with a devilish persistency? Sure! Then you vowed that henceforth you would proceed netless and beach 'em, only to encounter immediately thereafter that biggest trout of all, in a deep, dark pool, with beaching possibilities " forty miles away "— and you lost him! Right-o!

Any reader who, like the writer, ever has lost three landing-nets in four-seasons' trouting, will be interested to learn that a most serviceable article is

233

easily to be achieved at practically the cost of the netting itself and of a little time and easy labor, the chief requisite for the frame being a bit of discarded common telegraph-wire. In bending the wire to shape an iron vise is of assistance, likewise pliers, and some hard flat surface, like a piece of iron, to hammer the wire against.

For a short-handled frame, the whole seventeen inches long, make the handle part about five inches long and have the bow about eight inches at the extreme width. Make it somewhat triangular in shape with an almost straight front side. This is a good shape at any time but particularly advantageous for scooping up minnows. To this end also have the net fine-meshed; and make the frame double across the front so that one wire will serve as a guard to protect the lashing-cord against contact with bottom stones.

This net is light, effective, and it slips easily into the fishing-coat left pocket through the opening at the front edge of the garment. There it is securely carried, entirely out of the way, yet easily accessible when wanted. (By the way, we wonder if the reader is " wise " to those sleeveless fishing " coats," possessing all the advantages of the old-time article but ever so much cooler on a hot day.) If this net is dropped it will sink to the bottom and there is some chance of reclaiming it in running water. Or, for added security, a cord about three feet long

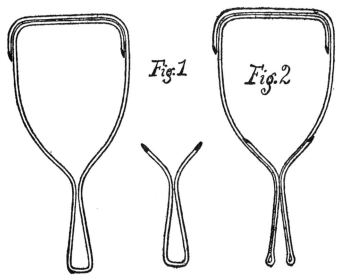

Showing how to put the frame together

may be tied to the handle and fastened at the other end to a coat buttonhole.

Two pieces of wire, bent in the forms shown in Fig. 1, are bound together with strong cord as illustrated in the photograph, the wire ends at the winding points being beveled with a file.

If a longer-handled net is desired, bend your two pieces of wire as shown in Fig. 2, bind together, and fasten to them a handle made from a piece of old broomstick, so that the whole is thirty-four inches long. The wire is riveted to the handle, a copper washer being next the wood at either side and also

outside the wire under the rivet head. Make the
openings for the rivet holes by bending the wire
around a nail and then jamming it up tight in an
iron vise, the jaws gripping close to the nail.   Have
the part of the handle that comes between the wires,
of a triangular, wedge shape — the back representing the base of the triangle — so that it will wedge
and hold firm when the handle is extended with the
net in use.   A buttonholed piece of leather is attached by a small brass screw, through a copper
washer, to the wooden handle just below the position
of the rivet, by means of which this form of net is
suspended from a button or hook that fastens the
left breast-pocket of your flannel shirt or is attached
in the vicinity of your left coat-lapel.   And the three-
foot piece of safety-cord may be used here also.

To prevent the net from dangling below the frame
when folded, fasten a loop of cord to the bottom of
the net, and slip this loop over the part of the
handle which projects beyond the rivet joint; it will
be checked at the leather hanger, but will release itself automatically when the handle is extended.

When either frame is completed, a coat of green
paint may be applied.

Now that this net problem is solved, let us consider for a little some other items of the angler's
equipment that make for safety and comfort.

Among these is a small rain-cape or poncho, that
will at least cover the shoulders but need not extend

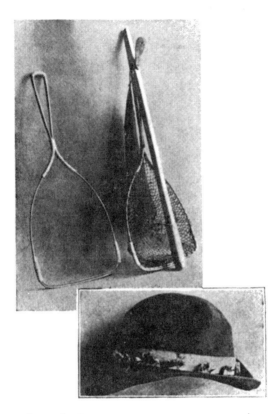

The author's net

Cravenetted (waterproof) hat with cork half-
disks sewed to band for carrying flies

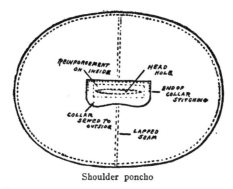

Shoulder poncho

much below the bend of the elbows. Such a garment
is easily fashioned.

Get two yards of five- or six-ounce close-woven
khaki duck, costing (when this was written) about
thirty cents a yard. Cut and sew it together as indicated on the accompanying diagram. Allow a little for seams, in cutting. The seam across the
center should be a lap-seam composed of the sel-
vedges. The edges at the circumference are hemmed.
After basting the halves together by hand, have the
seams and edges finished on a sewing-machine.
(Possibly you are on good enough terms with your
wife, or somebody else, to ask her.) The completed
cape is thirty-six inches from back to front, by forty-
four inches wide. It will reach to just below the
end of the elbow and does not interfere with casting. (While keeping it short in front it might be
lengthened to below the waist in the back, for better
protection when stooping or bending over.)

The center slit for the head is twelve and one-half inches long, and is sixteen and one-half inches from the front edge of the cape. It is reinforced by an extra piece of the goods three inches wide, sewed on the inside (shown in illustration). The edges of this piece and of the cape at the slit are turned in and sewed together.

Corresponding to this reinforcing piece but slightly larger, and sewed along but one edge — and half-way across at the ends — is the collar, three and one-half inches deep at the center and four inches at the ends. It is fastened to the outside of the cape as indicated by the dotted lines.

When the sewing is completed, melt one-quarter pound of paraffine shavings in a tin vessel (placed in a second vessel containing boiling water) and mix thoroughly with one pint of turpentine. Allow the whole to remain in the hot water bath, while applying it with a clean paint-brush to the outside of the cape. Dry the cape in the air. It may show streaky, but you can drive the paraffine into the cloth fiber and distribute it evenly by pressing the garment with a hot iron. A smaller proportion of melted beeswax sometimes is incorporated with the paraffine in such waterproofing operations.

Anyone with the least experience in camping will know of what paramount importance it is that you clothe yourself in woolen underwear. It need not be heavier than medium-weight, but it should be of wool. Even in midsummer it can be very chilly in the mountain altitudes that the angler haunts, after sundown especially; and it can be chilly at any time after a ducking in the stream, in the wind, with cotton next the skin. By the way, where the water is unusually treacherous, don't hesitate to cut a piece of sapling for a wading-staff.

Your hat should be an old felt one, with a brim for better protection from the sun and rain. This same paraffine solution will waterproof that hat too, but it will need a few ventilating windows at the sides; or it may be " cravenetted " or given a dose of lanolin. A handy thing to go around the hat is a leather or woven band to which cork half-disks are sewed for sticking flies into; or the band may have riveted to it strips of metal carrying little clips.

When next we shall have considered the angler's footwear, these include about all the essential articles of clothing that pertain especially to the fisherman; though we might add the general suggestion that no article of outer wear should contrast too strongly with his surroundings. This would give preference to such subdued colors as gray and yellowish- or greenish-browns.

To wear waders, or not to wear waders? Whether 't is best to discard them and get boldly wet, without any idea of trying to keep dry, or whether we shall encase ourselves within these air-excluding mackintoshes and stew in our own sweat

— regardless of the fact that one is almost certain to go " over the top "— that is the question.

There are three factors to be considered: foot-hold, dryness, and locomotion. If waders — either mackintoshes or hip-boots — are used, you must have hobnailed wading-brogans to wear over the feet of the one, or leather sandals with hobnailed soles or some similar contrivance for the feet of the other. Screw-calks are an advantage over hob-nails, which have a faculty of becoming loose and dropping out when the sole leather dries after long soaking. These calks may be transposed as re-quired, those wearing down quickest being moved to another part of the sole and replaced by some less worn. In addition to the woolen stockings next the skin, a heavier pair also are worn between wader and brogan, to ease the chafing of the former. These sometimes are turned into the tops of the brogans, making a double layer where the raw-hide lacings (keep them well greased) are drawn around the ankle at the tops of these shoes; but a better scheme, because keeping the sand from getting be-tween stocking and wader, is to pull the outside stockings up to full length and to secure the tops around the wader with a rubber-band. You can get these rubber-bands — and useful for so many other purposes — by cutting them from played-out auto-tire tubes.

The banana-peel can assume no airs in the presence

Cutting across country

The ford at high water

of a rock covered with slimy moss. A dangerous fall in or along the stream may prove no light matter for the lone angler, far from camp or farmhouse. A simple emergency expedient is to wrap strips of canvas or burlap or bind pieces of rope around the feet of rubber boots. Sand works into the meshes of the cloth and gives it a good gripping surface; or a pair of woolen socks may be worn over the boots — while they last.

Don't neglect to have along with you some kind of a rubber-patching outfit. These are sold by the tackle-man and also by rubber-goods people; the familiar tire-patches and cement will serve the purpose pretty well. Good waders cost money; we wonder why a fellow couldn't make something that would serve, of ten-ounce duck — patterning after an old pair of boughten goods — having lap-seams and being waterproofed with the beeswax, paraffine, and turpentine compound or something even better for the purpose.

Waders are all right — generally — when actually wading, but are cumbersome to walk in; besides, walking subjects them to excessive wear and tear. And, frequently, as much or more walking along stream is done as walking in the water. On the other hand, wading without waders is chilly business during early Spring fishing. The only solution here is to carry extra footwear in the shape of something light that can be slipped into when you desert the stream for a considerable hike over dry land, the while you hang the waders around your neck. For general hiking, the regulation Munson-last army shoes are the thing; and the dope for them is one, two, three parts respectively of resin, bees-wax, and mutton-tallow, melted together. Never dry out wet leather shoes by exposing them to too direct and strong fire-heat; fill them with hot sand or pebbles. Moccasins or felt slippers are a great comfort in camp.

Many veteran anglers have solved this wading problem, in a manner satisfactory to themselves at least. The early Spring fishing — except perhaps for very short snatches, and not too far removed from ready access to a good warm fire indoors — has long ceased to appeal to them very strongly; and ordinarily from the middle of May on they can keep very comfy without waders. They get right in, but keep moving and don't stop to rest at any time when there is the slightest suggestion of a chill. If camping, be sure to dry out thoroughly or change to warm, dry clothing before going to bed. The best stimulant after exposure is hot tea or hot black coffee, and warmth. Alcohol generally is better applied outside.

This reminds us that the hot-water bottle — of rubber or the canteen so used — comes in mighty handy when accident or sickness occurs in camp. You always can prepare the water, and the bottle filled with this and slipped under the patient's blanket may add much to his safety and comfort; or a hot stone wrapped in cloth may be utilized as a substitute. And the device isn't so bad for cold nights even for the camper who is perfectly well.

And don't forget that first-aid kit. It should include some compound cathartic pills or cascara laxative, two-grain capsules of muriate of quinine, five-grain aspirin tablets, " Sun " cholera tablets, a few two-inch gauze roller-bandages with small cartons of absorbent cotton and sterile gauze, tincture of iodine, some needles with catgut sutures in alcohol in tubes ready for use, a couple of artery clamps, some surgeons' plaster, and a hypodermic syringe with a few strychnine, cocaine, and morphine tablets for use with same. Before you leave home have a chat with your family doctor and make a memorandum of what he says about just when and how these things are to be used in an emergency. And though you probably will escape the necessity for the use of any of them for yourself or your immediate party, it is very satisfactory when you are enabled to play the " friend in need " to some member of another outfit or to some honest, whole-souled farmer, far from any source of prompt medical relief.

A mosquito-dope that is cleanly, and about as efficacious as any, is a mixture of one ounce each of creosote, oils of citronella and of pennyroyal, with

two ounces of olive or castor oil. The addition of
a tube of carbolated vaseline augments the wearing
quality. For some woods pests the incorporation
also of three ounces of pine tar increases efficacy,
but makes it much less pleasant to use. Mix by
heating the tar and olive or castor oil, then stir in the
other ingredients over a low fire until they are thoroughly incorporated. Two good and simple preparations are: two parts citronella, two parts spirits
of camphor, and one part oil of cedar; and, the other,
nine parts castor oil, eight parts sweet oil, two parts
carbolic acid, one part oil of pennyroyal. A fly-
dope in much favor with salmon-fishing guides of
the Gaspé country consists of equal parts of pine
tar and castor oil with the addition of a little bi-
sulphide of carbon. All these are good sunburn lo-
tions also.

Every article you read that tells about what to
take with you into the woods mentions the compass; but you do not see much note of the pedometer.
This inexpensive little instrument will add much to
the pleasure of your outing. It is easily adjusted to
your individual average length of step, is very reliable — as the writer has proven by checking up
with his auto odometer — and it is a satisfaction to
know distances definitely, as the length of certain
trails or exactly how far you are from the nearest
post-office, farmhouse, or some other point of special interest.

If not already informed, you will be glad to know about those government section-maps, to be had from the Department of the Interior, that note in great detail all the essential features of about almost any section of country that you may be planning to visit.

And don't overlook that flashlight, with extra batteries.

" J. A. C.", in *The American Angler*, tells about a friend who possessed " a barrel of tricks worth the attention of the angling fraternity. I was fishing the Concord River, Massachusetts, with him not long ago. It was raining; a bully day for fishing but a hard day for smoking, which is the special consolation of a wet day out of doors. He was in the bow of the canoe and I was trying to paddle just near enough to make good casting for both of us, myself fishing at the same time and trying to keep a pipe going too. Some job. Every once in a while I saw him lean over, open his coat and apparently scratch a match on the lining. It looked sensible to me, so I tried the same trick. But it didn't work. Finally, I asked him how he did it; the matches would n't light on the inside of my coat. He turned around, opened his coat toward me, and then I saw he had sewed onto the lining a *bit of rough emery-cloth,* about two inches wide by five inches long. ' Great scheme, Jim,' he said."

THE ANGLER'S CAMP

CHAPTER XIII

THE ANGLER'S CAMP

Where the silvery gleam of the rushing stream
Is so brightly seen o'er the rocks, dark green,
Where the white pink grows by the wild red rose
And the bluebird sings till the welkin rings;

Where the red deer leaps and the panther creeps,
And the eagles scream over cliff and stream,
Where the lilies bow their heads of snow,
And the hemlocks tall throw a shade o'er all;

Where the rolling surf laves the emerald turf,
Where the trout leaps high at the hovering fly,
Where the sportive fawn crops the soft green lawn,
And the crows' shrill cry bodes a tempest nigh —
    There is my home — my wildwood home.

Where no steps intrude in the dense dark wood,
Where no song is heard but of breeze and bird;
Where the world's foul scum can never come;
Where friends are so few that all are true —
    There is my home — my wildwood home.
            —EDWARD Z. C. JUDSON ("Ned Buntline")
            (An Adirondack camp in ante-bellum days)

Angling leads naturally to camping, because of
the manifest advantage of being domiciled most conveniently to the waters to be fished; and though con-
scious of the plethora of printed advice upon the subject of camp-life and equipment, we yet have the

hardihood to believe we may be able to " hand out " a few pointers that will prove neither redundant nor altogether devoid of practical value to many of our readers.   There are things about this outdoor game that it is not possible to overemphasize.

Whenever you project a camping trip, take it for granted that you are going to camp *in the rain*. To be sure, it may not rain — but then, again, it does.   If you are prepared for it, you yet can have a satisfactory trip; if you are not, it is absolutely and irretrievably spoiled.   The first consideration is to have your tents actually — not supposedly — waterproof, especially their roofs; and if for an extended trip, have an additional roof-piece or " fly " to spread a few inches above the tent roof proper.

Of course one does not expect to go upon such an expedition in the middle of June, in this latitude, and encounter two weeks of the coolest and wettest weather that the Weather Bureau has turned loose in over forty years for a corresponding period. And yet if one of the chief features of the trip was to be the testing of the practical qualifications of a little homemade shelter-tent, no one may deny that the weather served the purpose admirably.— Wherefore the story of the tent that " made good."

The place is the upper waters, in Sullivan County, N. Y., of a little river that for recommendation has size, beauty, and wildness in great variety, freedom

ANGLERS' CAMP

to angle for miles without interference, and the presence of many trout in its waters, both native and brown, averaging a goodly size, requiring skill to attach, and never in primer condition then during this season, the early Summer of 1916.

The modest intention of the author, and designer of the aforesaid tent, was to produce a creation that should embody all the good points of all the good tents that had preceded it — and then some. Whether or not he succeeded in this particular endeavor, the tent proved a success all right; with the addition of a butler's pantry and garage it almost might pass for a Newport summer cottage.

It is seven feet square on the ground, seven feet to the peak at the top of the triangular front side, and has an eighteen-inch wall at the back. It has windows fifteen by eighteen inches, screened by cheesecloth, and provided with flaps outside, adjusted by cords; and the door in the front is five feet high above a six-inch sill, three feet wide at the bottom, and fourteen inches at top. This opening a'so is protected by a cheesecloth screen-door which draws to one side and is gathered by tapes when not in use, and also there is a regular flap-door, hinged at the top and secured when closed by large hooks-and-eyes. (De Long " Jumbos." The same likewise fasten the sleeping-bag flaps, presently to be no'ed.)

The bottom and one side of the door-space, to

which the screen-door is not sewed, is made in *double flaps between which* the free edges of the screen-door are secured with safety-pins in closing it. Edges of screen-door are bound with tape. The outer door may be entirely closed, be stayed out in front like that of a Frazer canoe-tent, or be closed at either side with the opposite side held open. A small piece of sapling is run through a pocket at the top edge of the door-sill to prevent sagging.

The material is the best quality unbleached muslin — about twenty-five yards of it — tanned by immersion in a hot decoction of ground white oak bark. (Another time we believe we will go in for a green color, with "Diamond" household-dye, and will use the government airplane cloth, beautiful for tents.) The muslin was passed through the solution three times, rinsed each time, and hung out to dry (thereby greatly arousing the curiosity of the neighbors). This before cutting. The proportion for the dye, as given by Kephart, was two pounds of the dry ground-bark to three and one-half gallons of water. After chipping the bark into small pieces with a hatchet it was ground in a hand grist-mill. When dry, the muslin was waterproofed by the alum and lead method. This consists in preparing two solutions, one with three-quarters of a pound of alum and the other with the same amount of sugar (acetate) of lead, each of which is dissolved in four gallons of boiling soft water. When dissolved, and clear, pour first the alum solution and then the lead water together into another vessel. Allow this to stand for several hours to deposit sediment, then pour off the clear liquid say into the washtub. Soak and knead the fabric in this, let it stand an hour or two, rinse in clear water, and hang out in the air to dry, without wringing. This makes not only a pretty effective waterproofing but mildew-proofs the cloth, and to no little extent renders it spark proof.

The weight of the tent material without the ground-cloth is a little over five pounds.

From past experience the writer holds strong convictions that the stretcher form of bed is at once the most generally practical and comfortable for camping, so he decided to incorporate stretcher-bed accommodations for two in the ground-cloth, which is sewed to the bottom edges of the tent all the way around. (Yes, madam, this will keep out wriggly and crawly things.) Also he decided to provide flaps for these beds, to hold the blankets in place. Furthermore, the tent-bottom, in addition to thus serving as *combined ground-cloth, stretcher-beds, and sleeping-bags,* also was to be the waterproof cover for the whole outfit, when packed; and could be utilized as a packsack in which to carry additional duffle, as a hatchet or small ax, folding reflector-baker, an army intrenching-tool or a miniature shovel; and last but not least, a half-dozen old newspapers. All this, and in addition two single five-pound army-blankets, which are laid out flat inside the tent, on the floor — for packing — and folded within it. Thus the tent can be raised in a rain-storm without getting a drop of wet on the bedding.

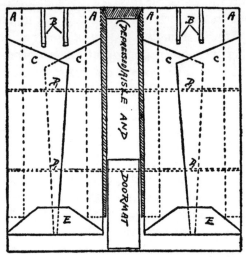

Ground-plan of combined tent ground-cloth, stretcher-beds, and sleeping-bags: A — Stretcher-pole pockets; B — Pillow straps; C, E — Sleeping-bag flaps; D — Lap-seams

The ground-cloth, complete as described, and waterproofed by the paraffine method, is made of regulation army ten-ounce khaki duck, three widths of which laid crosswise of the ground-plan, came out just right after allowing for the lapped seams. About eleven yards were required.

In applying the paraffine, about a pound was cut into shavings and melted on the stove, removed and added to two-quarts of gasolene, on the roof (more incitement of neighbors' curiosity — almost painful), the whole kept warm and fluid by placing it in a basin of hot water. The ground-cloth then was spread out and the paraffine and gasolene mixture applied hot to the bottom side with a paint-brush. It congealed in streaks as soon as applied. Then it was hung in the sun and air (neighbors forgotten by this time) for three or four hours, and finally was ironed with a very hot iron, care being taken not to burn it, which gave a uniform, smooth result, spreading the paraffine evenly all over and into the fabric.

Some prefer to mix the paraffine with turpentine, and yet again, a small quantity of melted beeswax sometimes is added. Also there are ready-prepared waterproofing solutions, such as "Preservo," etc., which you can buy at the camp outfitter's for from a dollar up per gallon. Another waterproofing process for cotton goods, consists in working pure linseed oil thoroughly into it with a brush. As applied to a tent, first set it up with everything pulling even and taut, and start at the ridge or top and work toward the ground. The tent must be left up, well exposed to sun and air, for two or three weeks before folding it for packing or storage.

In utilizing the stretcher-bed feature of our tent — though it may be used as an ordinary tent, without this — four saplings, about two and one-half

inches at the butt and about nine feet long, are thrust
through five-inch-wide pockets sewed on the under-
side of the ground-cloth (for the middle pockets, the
others being made by folding the edges under) and
extending from the back of the tent to within about
a foot of the front edge; a pocket along either side
of the middle, about sixteen inches apart.   This left
a center aisle, which by sewing in two triangular side
gores and a rectangular piece at the back, gave a
trough or gutter between the two beds when the beds
were raised at the head about ten inches above the
ground, at the back of the tent.   The front ends of
the stretcher-poles simply were embedded in the
ground, flush with the surface, and held apart here
by stakes driven into the ground flush with their top
sides.   Thus one can stand or walk on the canvas
of the center aisle with the solid ground underfoot,
when the rear ends of the poles are elevated.

In setting up, the beds are stretched taut sideways,
and the poles held apart at the back, by large nails
driven against their sides and into a thicker, cross-
pole resting upon stones and atop of which the
stretcher-poles are supported.   They project about
two feet beyond the tent rear wall.   This arrangement is shown in the photo of the rear of the tent,
as also are the extension-flaps at bottom of back and
sides of the tent which prevent wind from blowing
under the beds when used as stretcher-beds.

In any form of bed off the ground, the camper

1—Inside of author's tent, showing stretcher-bed with flaps and
    blanket, pillow, window, and pockets
2—Rear view, with stretcher-beds in use

must guard against *cold from underneath* — that's where the chill principally comes from. Banking up around the sides with earth and sod, and even a thin layer of balsam, hemlock, or pine fans placed between the canvas of the bed and the blanket will materially help here.

Of course these stretcher-beds are bound to sag some, but to insure comfortable results you hollow out the ground under the middle of each bed, a little distance each way from where your hips come, and for a space about eighteen inches wide by three feet long. The old army intrenching-tool does this work handily and serves well the purpose of camp shovel, in ditching tents, etc.

A tent invariably should be well ditched, and its site should be selected with special reference to water draining away from it in the event of heavy rains; also with due regard to convenience of drinking water and firewood. And don't pitch your tent directly *under* large trees, particularly dead ones, or ones with dead limbs that might be blown down by the wind and endanger your life. Nearby trees are all right, to serve as a windbreak in the protection of which your camp is pitched, but the site should be well exposed to the sun for a part of the day. The ditch generally should extend around all four sides of your tent, should be nearly a foot deep, and a leader ditch should connect with the low corner. A more effective ditch-digger than the in-

trenching-tool is a folding or collapsible shovel.   It
is a mighty handy instrument about camp — so is
a small cross-cut saw.

Plenty of trouble, perhaps you are thinking, for
the sake of comfortable sleeping.   Well, son, when
your uncle is out on a two-weeks' camping trip, if
there is one thing that he 's going to do it is to sleep
comfortably or he will know the reason why.   It
is the novice at the game whose specialty is " rough-
ing it."   Your true woodsman certainly has learned
to accommodate his wants to restricted means, but
he is the last man to submit himself needlessly to
harmful exposure and privation.   And say, speaking of trouble, did ever you attempt to make one of
those all-browse affairs? — make it right and keep
it so?   That *is* work.   And did we sleep comfortably in our stretcher-beds? — *Did* we?   Ask " Denny
the Axman," sixty-three years young and good for
a twenty-mile hike any day — he 'll answer.

In using this tent for only a night or two, the
stretcher-bed feature need not be utilized; the tent
being set up with the bottom flat and laid over
leaves, browse, or grass.   In this way it easily will
sleep three adults.   Used for two, luxuriating in
the stretcher-beds, there is the aisle affording room
for a small boy or for storage of considerable duffle,
and also a space at the foot of each bed, as the beds
are six inches less than the full length of the tent.
" Next time " we shall increase this fore-and-aft

length of the tent perhaps a foot, to gain more stor-
age-room at this convenient spot.

One may stand at full height well within the door
of this canvas woods-dwelling, for changing clothes,
etc., and he has headroom to sit up in his bed; yet
the walls are so steep that a good quality of unbleached muslin, treated as stated, proved effectively
waterproof, even if the material was rubbed against
on the inside. And our house is *well ventilated,*
both because of the windows and as the alum and
lead process does not seal the pores of the cloth
while conferring protection from the wet. The
writer and his tent-mate " Denny "— and may every
camper have his equal for wearing qualities —
weathered on this trip a continuous thirty-six-hour
downpour which raised the river twenty-two inches,
higher than it reached in early Spring.

But not yet have we exhausted the catalog of the
virtues of this little tent. On the inside of its rear
wall are four pockets, and there are two more on
either side-wall, alongside the heads of the beds, for
miscellaneous articles of clothing, etc. The curious
" swellings " of the accompanying illustrations show
that they were appreciatively utilized.

Across the top edge of the rear wall and from
thence extending from the rear corners to the peak
is a continuous piece of braided cotton-rope, with
small galvanized thimbles at these corners. This
rope-triangle bears all the chief strain of the ropes

holding the tent, and it is sewed to the inside of the roof at its edges. About two feet from the peak it is left unattached for a space to admit of the insertion of a pothook for suspension of a Stonebridge folding candle-lantern (never go into camp without one, and use the extra hard plumbers'-candles that will burn for hours with a minimum of drip).

The main guy-ropes are two single ropes leading from the top corners of the low rear wall, and a much longer double rope leading from the peak over a pair of sapling shears and secured at either side out in front; and the shears leave the door unobstructed. By easy manipulation of these shears and of the *tautening-sticks* placed under the rear guys, slack quickly is taken up when required.

The weight of the completed ground-cloth is about ten pounds, making fifteen or sixteen pounds for the completed tent; and twenty-five or -six pounds for the whole outfit, including ten pounds of blankets, which one man readily may carry in a packstrap while his companion lugs the cook-kit and the grub.

Oh, about those newspapers! The added weight is insignificant, and spread out between the blanket and the canvas, under and over the sleeper, they are effective for much added warmth in chilly weather. During prolonged wet weather you will appreciate more than ever the value of woolen underwear for the woods, even in Summer; and also the desirability of a warm, dry, comfortable bed. Sheepskin bed-slippers are another great comfort; so is a sleeping-hood at times. Another pointer on the theme of keeping warm in extra chilly weather: The time that most you will feel the cold is about three A. M., and the place will be your back, between waist and shoulders. A sheepskin vest may be bought for four or five dollars and is a good investment — either way you look at it; and it's nice for automobiling in Winter, especially for the doctor when he gets up out of a warm bed in the early hours to face the chill blast. If, in addition to the observance of these suggestions, you carry to bed with you the hot-water bottle mentioned in the previous chapter, and should you chance to have along a down quilt to curl up in inside your blanket — well, you may realize that you can be comfortable even in a tent, in the woods, and in the rain. Of course it requires fore-thought and the application of brains and ingenuity; and while the latter may be some other fellow's or a composite of some other outdoorsmen's, *the fore-thought must be yours.* Down quilts, though un-deniably bulky, are extremely light; and you can economize both in bulk and cost by dividing one full-sized quilt into three parts, each of which will afford good back protection for one sleeper; or a feather pillow will serve as the makings of such a pad. For very severe weather, though, there is nothing in the tent line equal to one in the baker style, left open in front, and whose slanting back-wall reflects down on its occupants the heat from a good fire built out in front.

Other little details of our tent are a doormat (yes, sir!) made of an extra piece of duck, fifteen inches by three feet, secured at the front of the aisle just within the door by hooks-and-eyes, to save the ground-cloth proper from muddy feet; and two straps sewed at the head of each bed under which

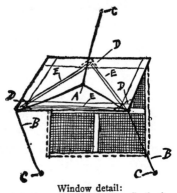

Window detail:
A — Cord and bridle for raising flap. B — Cords for guys and closing. C — Eyelet-holes through tent wall. D — Triangular pockets at back and corners to insert: E — Twigs to reinforce flap.

to slip the pillows so they will stay put, said pillows consisting of flour-bags stuffed with reserve under-wear, etc., or with balsam or other evergreen tips or even ordinary leaves, moss, or grass.   Mention also should be made here of the little pockets at the back and at the front corners of the window-flaps, for the insertion of twigs to hold these shutters out

Side view of author's tent

Baker tent

flat when raised. The adjusting-cords lead through buttonholed eyelets to the inside of the tent and are secured as desired by making a slip-noose in them, the knot of which lies against the inside wall close against the eyelet holes. We believe, gentlemen, we have only to mention that along the line of direct strain at the sides of the triangle forming the front wall, and from the top of the rear wall along each side to the ground front-corners of this paragon of a tent, the muslin is reinforced by three-quarter inch tape sewed on the inside.

This tent is erected, except for the finer details, simply by staking out the four ground corners, and then carrying the front guys from the peak over the shears — thus it very quickly is made a " safe port in a storm." The procedure was to chuck all our other dunnage immediately into this and next to erect the big fly (see ahead); we then could arrange the further camp details under cover, at leisure. Our regular outfit comprises in addition two other, seven by seven wall tents and the duffle-bags.

An important point in the construction of any real tent is that it should have eaves, projecting at least two or three inches, where the roof meets the side-wall at a sharp angle, and especially when a seam is there; another thing is that it often is a good stunt to economize in weight by having the sides of very light material but to have the *roof* of heavier stuff.

A simpler application of the stretcher-bed principle makes at once the easiest to erect, lightest, and most comfortable form of temporary night-shelter known to the writer. All you need is a single stretcher-bed canvas (they are stocked in the out-fitting shops), a poncho or similar square of water-proof material, and a blanket; or a second poncho with two edges grommeted to lace together may be used over the stretcher-bed poles. You cut two saplings for these stretcher poles; and four more, smaller poles with which to make two pairs of shears, about four feet high and with a three-foot base.

Stretcher-bed temporary shelter

The shears are driven into the ground about four and one-half feet apart. The stretcher-poles lie *outside* the shears, elevated enough to clear the ground nicely. As the weight of the stretcher occupant then tends to spread his bed, it automatically is kept taut. A rope serves as ridge and at the same time stays the whole thing at the ends, where it is securely staked

— have all main tent-stakes strong and *long* enough
to hold when that big wind arrives in the dead of
some night.   The poncho or whatnot is thrown over
the ridge-rope — and that's all there is to it.

Remember then, when you are preparing your
woodland couch, to *get clear of the ground.*   Next
to some such affair, the best thing to do is to scoop
out a full-length hole, at least six or eight inches
deep, fill this with browse level with the ground, and
then to top this with your damp-excluding poncho
within which is folded your blanket.

If the personnel of your party is large enough
for two or more tents, a nice thing is to have a large
waterproof fly that you can use for the ridged roof
of a court around three sides of which the tents are
grouped, each facing the center.   Such an arrangement makes a very comfortable "fix."   In pro-
tracted rainy weather you can build your small cooking-fire under this large fly and sit around it and
eat in comfort; also you have the means of drying
out clothing, etc.   Upon our trip mentioned above
we had a sixteen-foot-square fly for this purpose,
which, stretched over and between our tents, proved a
life saver; this also was treated with the alum and
lead, but it is of six-ounce drill.   We had pitched
camp in the rain, most of the time continued to camp
in the rain, and all but broke camp in the rain.   You
may keep dry during a prolonged rainy season and
yet find the confinement of close tent-life very irk-

some; a device of the kind we have described adds much to your freedom of movement under these circumstances. In the picture of the "Anglers' Camp" you will see how three tents may be set up around such a big central fly. It had best extend a little beyond the front of each tent, being about two feet higher than the tents at their highest point; the open side of the court faces the stream. Here is a rough diagram of the plan. The uprights which support the ridge-pole for this big fly may also be utilized in the erection of two of the tents.

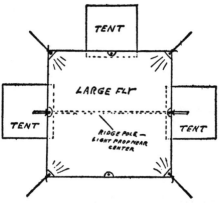

Plan of tents grouped to face central court roofed by large fly

Another thing that will add measurably to your comfort in a wet camp is some pieces of canvas with which you may improvise stools and chairs to sit upon under cover of your fly. A triangular piece of duck, twelve to fifteen inches long on the sides, rope-bound and looped at the corners — or hemmed at the edges and reinforced at the corners, where grommets are inserted — with the blunt-pointed ends of three crossed sticks thrust into these corners, the sticks being bound together at the middle, makes a stool not to be sneezed at.

Before we proceed any further with this discussion we must have special concern for our matches. If you have but once experienced the feeling of miserable desolation in the wet woods without the means of producing that thing most desirable of all, the cheer of a fire, you need not be impressed with the idea that those matches must be stored in an absolutely water-tight tin receptacle. A shaving-stick metal holder makes a handy one. And it is n't a bad stunt always to have on your person a special, emergency supply of matches further protected by previously having had their heads dipped in shellac or melted paraffine.

Moreover don't overlook the value of a store of dry, small pine-kindlings — mere slivers of wood that you bring from home, included amongst your duffle, and guard jealously by taking them to bed with you, under the blanket, and reserve strictly for actual need. The war-introduced " trench torch " or candle is also a great boon when starting a fire under dam(p), bad circumstances.

Some of these things we have discussed thus far are in truth but the A B C's of the expert woodsman, but soon we are about to reveal something that we believe to be really new — at any rate very little known — about camp-fires; in short we now shall discourse about the " Loot's " rain-defying outside camp-fire, a discovery that he made on our memorable wet expedition, demonstrating before our very eyes how necessity could be the mother of invention. This phenomenon is that of keeping a fire going right out in the open, *and with a good steady rain raining right along!* As already affirmed, so far as we are aware the inspiration of genius that created it had its genesis in the cerebrum of Charlie, the popular Lieutenant, as intimated, of our local branch of the State Guard, and one of our Westchester County Supervisors. If he supervises the county affairs that directly concern Yonkers as ably as he can supervise a camp-fire, he should be elected to succeed himself perennially.

After a fire is once well started under cover it is a simple enough matter to dry out alongside of it firewood for use as needed — and if you are not an experienced camper you will be astonished to learn how small a cooking-fire need be to be efficient; it 's that starting it that may be the rub, to say nothing of keeping it going satisfactorily in the open. So to start this Charlie affair a-going, you may have to hunt for some dry tinder from the inside of a dead stump or log. Or the thin outer bark of the white or yellow birches contains a vegetable oil that will

admit of its being fired even when sodden with wet.
(Birch logs are the best-burning green wood.) But
you must proceed in the right way. Make a cy-
lindrical roll of this bark, stand it vertically with
the lower edge resting on two small stones or pieces
of wood to lift it at least an inch clear of the ground,
brace it thus with a few small pieces of kindling
ranged about it conewise, like the poles of a miniature tepee tent, and fire the bark at the bottom edge.
In addition to birch-bark, you should lose no time
in collecting a stock of small, dry, dead twigs for
safe storage in camp after it is once pitched, for
kindling, against a wet spell, and occasionally you
may souse these with surplus frying-pan fat. These
or your pine kindlings and your birch-bark will furnish sufficient nucleus for a good fire at any time.
If you have thought to bring along a small bellows,
so much the better. A piece of rubber tubing attached to a short metal tube having one end flat-
tened to insinuate under the embryo fire (perhaps
made from an old rod-ferrule), isn't a bad fire-
blower. (The whole might easily be fashioned
from a doctors' defunct stethoscope.)

But how did Charlie do it? — well, we're getting
to that. His beautiful idea is to build a roof of wet
firewood over the fire, by placing one end of the
sticks on the top backlog, butting against a strip of
wood stood vertically to keep them from slipping
off, with their forward ends resting on the cross-bar

or crane from which the pots and " kittles " are suspended, and projecting somewhat in front of it. A
little space is left between the sticks as they are
laid side by side, so they will not blanket the fire
too much. These screen the fire from the rain sufficiently so that it will keep burning, and the fire
dries them enough so that they burn readily. When
the fire needs replenishing you feed it with a piece
of the roof dropped dry side down, and replace this
with another, wet piece of firewood; how 's that for
perpetual reciprocity!

But after all, what less should we have expected
as a result of Charlie's exuberant personal and professional qualifications! I have mentioned something about his social and political activities — but
not a word as to his business-card, which in our home
paper reads as follows:

> Secure our estimate on your heating
> plant (new or repairs). Our work
> and materials give the best service.
> Our figures are close.
> **W———— & C————**
> Steam and Water Heating

The unanimous vote of the bunch at " Big-Birch "
camp was that his services were eminently satisfactory, and that the result of his " figuring " was beyond cavil as economical of time and energy as the
above literary specimen is devoid of verbiage.

In the accompanying illustration of this arrangement there is no camouflage about the trout frying

A RAIN-DEFYING OUTSIDE CAMP-FIRE

in the pan, although the " panhandler " in this instance is not the fire and county supervisor, but
" Denny the Axman," who more recently has mani-
fested an ambition to " usurp " the cook's preroga-
tives.

Every orthodox camp outfit must include a " ditty-
bag "— a compact collection of things of general
utility.   Here are some of the items that should
not be overlooked.   We already have mentioned
nails, in connection with the tent stretcher-bed.
They are most useful in camp; have on assortment
of varied sizes, and including hobnails.   A ball of
marlin is handy for lashing tent-poles, etc.   *Pliers*
and a coil of *wire* often are not to be despised.   Of
course you want *sewing materials,* including thimble
or a sailmakers' palm, beeswax, and patches and but-
tons, for clothing and tent repairs.   *Tackle- and
wader-repairing outfits* must find a place.   A *leather-
stitching hand awl* may not come amiss.   Then there
is that *file* and *carborundum-stone* for sharpening the
ax and other edged tools.   And don't forget *safety-
pins* — fine for pinning shirt-pockets so things won't
drop out; and big fellows, horse-blanket size, are just
as good for blankets for humans — to pin fast the
doubled-up bottom, when you arrange it in sleeping-
bag style, and for holding the top in place.

The ax itself won't go into the ditty-bag — for,
in addition to the camp hatchet or small ax, you want
a real ax for real execution; it should be at least

a " three-quarter " size.   But it will pack all right into the center of a duffle-bag, the blade having a guard affixed.   That icemen's ax, with its pick at one end of the head, isn't a bad camp-tool, with the handle shortened.   And it is a good idea to wire your ax- and hatchet-heads to their helves, by inserting a piece of stout wire through a hole bored through the handle close to the back of the head and then bringing the ends of the wire in front of the head and twisting them together.

The novice will be interested to see what an actual " grub-list," ample for five men for two weeks, will look like.   We lived royally on this with the addition to the ménu of trout, wild-strawberry shortcake, and some potatoes and a fowl or two obtained from a farmer — in a manner perfectly legitimate. And note that we were not unmindful of the value of macaroni as a portable potato-substitute.   The total expense of this trip, exclusive of railroad fares but inclusive of twelve dollars paid for the transportation of the whole outfit, men and dunnage, into and out of the woods — about twenty-five miles — at the prices then current, amounted to seventy-nine cents per day for each member of the party. Alas! those days so recent yet of yore have gone, never to return.   Here then follows the larder:

7 pounds flour	4 pounds rice
4 pounds prepared pancake-flour	10 pounds bacon
	2 pounds salt pork

"COME GET IT"—and it seems to be drying day

2 pounds cornmeal
4 pounds beans
2 pounds lima beans
2 pounds split peas
8 packages spaghetti
1 pot mustard
5 pounds cheese .
3 pounds hardtack
6 pounds onions
1 package Pettijohn
3 packages H. O.
5 pounds butter
½ pound baking powder
7 pounds coffee
1 pound tea
4 cans cocoa
14 cans unsweetened evaporated milk

1 can Crisco
12½ pounds sugar
1 pound salt
1 box pepper
4 nutmegs
8 cans soup
4 pounds dried prunes
2 pounds dried apricots
5 pounds raisins
24 Steero beef-cubes
12 cakes German's sweet chocolate
2 pounds English walnuts
3 jars mixed pickles
8 jars jams and jellies
2 jars honey
1 bottle salad dressing

(*Note.*—Powdered milk, as the "Klim" brand, may be substituted for condensed milk in liquid form. Dehydrated vegetables, such as potatoes and onions, and dehydrated berries are worth keeping in mind. Sugar, flour, coffee, and tea are best first enclosed individually in paraffined muslin bags, and salt in a wooden box to keep it dry. In packing jars of jelly, etc., wrap in newspapers and then put in empty tobacco-cans, securing the covers with strips of adhesive plaster on which mark the contents. Generally you may check on the railroad as baggage 150 pounds of properly packed dunnage to each man.)

For a nutritious emergency ration in compact form, to carry in the pocket when away from camp for the day, have some rolled-wheat cereal (as Pettijohn's), dry raisins, walnut meats, German's sweet chocolate (Walter Baker and Co.), and a little tea. You can pit some prunes and insert the walnut meats — which make prunes acceptable to anyone. Then there is that concentrated form of pulverized coffee (G. Washington brand). Carry these in a little paraffined-muslin bag. Also take along on these little side-trips some bits of trench torch; one piece supplies sufficient fire to heat water or make coffee. These torches are made by rolling newspapers into a tight cylinder of about an inch in diameter, pasting the outside sheet to hold all, sawing into two- or three-inch lengths, and then boiling them for five minutes in paraffine. Or you can make them of burlap or any coarse cloth soaked in most any grease.

It is quite desirable that your provisions be protected from the depredations of ants and other woods pests, prominent among which is the porcupine. Effectual against crawling vermin will be the simple expedient of making a skeleton table of small boughs, having legs about a foot long to raise it above the ground. Have each leg resting in a tin can, fill the cans with water, and store your provisions on this table in the commissary tent. A securer plan is to store them upon a covered shelf suspended in mid-air by wire attached to a horizontal limb of a tree.

Have everything neat as a pin about your camp, burying all refuse that won't burn. You inevitably will leave behind unmistakable signs of having camped in the spot, but don't expose yourselves to the diagnosis of having "picnicked" there. Every true lover of the woods is scrupulously careful about the disposition of lighted matches, and about quenching all fires after they have served his purpose; the Game Commission and the Forest Service have not

harped upon this precaution one bit too much.
In addition to the grub, also the following items,
some not already noted, were on my checking-list:

Cheap canvas gloves, used in
  handling the reflector-baker
Canteen
Collapsible canvas-bucket
Cook-kit
Pipes and tobacco
Mosquito-dope
Three-in-One oil
18 candles
Flour-bag pillow-slips
Mirror
Postal cards
Indelible pencil
Whisk-broom
Map
Compass
Pedometer

File
Carborundum-stone
Camera and films
Flashlight and extra batteries
Hot-water bag
Bellows
Pine kindlings
Canvas stool-seats
Medicine-kit
  4 boxes matches
  2 cakes Babbitt's soap
  2 cakes Ivory soap
  1 cake Sapolio
  1 can Greosolvent hand-paste
  1 box toothpicks
Bird, tree, and flower books
Calendar

Note this last item; it is surprising in how short
a time in the woods you can lose all track of the
days.

Fresh-water fish that you intend to ship or trans-
port home are best cleaned soon after killing; this
should include removal of the gills but not of the
large blood-sinus along the backbone. You may
place inside each fish some damp watercress (not
ferns or grass); wrap individually and tightly in
paraffined or other paper to exclude the air; and
then make of all one package wrapped in sawdust
and more paper, and cloth — dry. Till the last
moment before shipment or transportation, keep

them if possible on but not against ice; otherwise keep in a covered pail buried in the ground or set in a shallow, shady part of the stream. This latter way we have kept trout in camp perfectly sweet and firm for over three days in midsummer. Fresh fish are also sometimes packed in salt for a journey, which is soaked out in water at their destination, before cooking them; and yet another plan is to hang them in the smoke of the camp-fire a few hours, after gutting them, and then wrap after they are plentifully peppered inside.

To clean trout, sever the attachment of the gills well forward under the lower jaw and at the sides in front of the pectoral fins; hook your finger into the gills and strip toward the tail, when everything comes away clean at once. The nicest way to prepare bass is, after scaling, to cut along each side of the dorsal fin the whole length of the back, with a good-sized sharp knife, and carrying the incision across the body behind the gill covers; then " saw " off a steak or fillet close down to the bones, discarding the rest. Pickerel and perch preferably are skinned.

The safest place to carry your bill-roll is in a chamois-leather bag securely fastened around your neck.

Keep a notebook of choice bits of practical information on camping, woodcraft, and angling acquired on your trips into the woods.

STILL YOUNG—IN ENTHUSIASM

A last caution — which might well have come first — is that you be wary of your drinking supply when camping. If you imbibe the nectar of the gods from a living spring at its source —" b'gosh, that's the kind er water a feller kin drink when he ain't dry!"— you should n't worry. But if in the least suspicious of contamination, either boil the water or treat it with a dilute solution of chloride of lime. The following formula will be satisfactory: Add one teaspoonful of fresh chloride of lime to one pint of water, which will keep for several days if stored in a stoppered bottle. If one teaspoonful of *this solution* is added to *two gallons* of drinking water and allowed to stand for half an hour the water will then be safe for use.

But my! boys, it's getting late; and the camp-fire has burned low. Suppose we all crawl into our blankets. Good night! and a full creel for everybody tomorrow.

Finally, patient " Scholer," and once again,

> Here's to the swish of the Split-Bamboo! —
> Musical swish of *your own* bamboo.—

Go to it! And may the abounding benediction of the Great Father of the beautiful outdoors be visited upon each and every one of you, in the guise of renewed brightness of eye, elasticity of step, acceleration of appetite and digestion coincident with reduction of equatorial girth, refreshment of slumber, serenity of mind, and mellowness of heart, so long as warbling birds, Springtime flowers, the whispering woods, and murmuring waters shall exist for our periodical enchantment and sanctuary — which may it be a long, long while, before, joining my old-time angling companion John P——, we too will have passed on, out of sight downstream, to that faraway land where " a pure river of the Water of Life, clear as crystal, proceedeth from the throne of God."

Make all good men your well-wishers,
   and then, in the years' steady sifting,
Some of them turn into friends. Friends
   are the sunshine of life.
                        — JOHN HAY.

OTHER APPLEWOOD TITLES YOU WILL ENJOY

The Gospel of Nature
John Burroughs

In 1912, America's great naturalist John Burroughs
was asked by a preacher to talk to his people on
the "gospel of nature." In this response, Burroughs
focused on what gave him solace and strength
4 x 6½, 48 pp., $5.95

Walking
Henry David Thoreau

Walking, now again considered to be an important form of
exercise, was the activity from which Thoreau continually
examined man's relationship with nature.
4¾ x 6⅝, 64 pp., $6.95

The Official Handbook for Boys
Boy Scouts of America

A facsimile reprint of the first *Boy Scout Handbook*,
complete with the original advertisements. More than
31 million copies of the *Boy Scout Handbook*
have been distributed since the first edition in 1911.
5 x 7¼, 416 pp., $14.95

APPLEWOOD BOOKS, P.O. Box 365, Bedford, MA 01730